Primary Science and Literacy

▶ Rosemary Feasey

PUBLISHED BY THE ASSOCIATION FOR SCIENCE EDUCATION

**Published by the Association for Science
Education, College Lane, Hatfield,
Herts AL10 9AA**

Tel: 01707 283000
Fax: 01707 266532

ASE web site on-line sales: www.ase.org.uk/products/
ASE book sales email: timbarrett@ase.org.uk

Edited by **Helen Johnson**
Designed by **Colin Barker**

Printed by Streets Printers, Royston Road,
Baldock, SG7 6NW

ISBN 0 86357 296 0

© The Association for Science Education, 1999

Contents

Preface

Science and literacy are inextricably linked. Without personal literacy individual children will find it more difficult to engage with science and certainly doors to a range of literature, both fiction and non-fiction, will be closed. Society needs literate people who are also scientifically literate; the two together enable people both individually and collectively to engage with a democratic system which enables people to contribute to science either directly or indirectly.

Some people become research scientists. Others become amateur scientists: for example, astronomers, many of whom have made important contributions to our knowledge of the universe. Others use science in their everyday jobs or leisure pursuits. In a society where the written and oral word explodes on to screens, airwaves and paper, one might be as bold as to suggest that to be a literate individual is one's birthright as much as food, water, shelter, love and safety.

The partnership between science and literacy is two way: science offers natural contexts for the use and development of literacy skills and understanding whilst literacy helps to offer the individual access to the exciting and challenging world of science.

My thanks are due to colleagues who gave their time so willingly to help produce this book. They include Jenny Cumming, Christine Davidson and Sylvia Hope.

A special thanks to all the teachers who so generously replied to my appeal for children's work for the book. It illustrates that the ASE really is *'Teachers helping teachers to teach science'*.

Rosemary Feasey

September 1998

Acknowledgements

Many people have kindly supported the production of this book. In listing the generous help provided by the following, my sincere apologies to any I have inadvertently omitted.

ASE Primary Science Committee

Ashley Road Primary School, Tyneside

Calton Junior School, Gloucester

Cilffriw Primary School, Neath

Cleadon Junior School, Tyneside

Copthorne First School, Bradford

Cunningham Hill Infant School, St Albans

Downsell Primary School, London

Grange Park Primary School, Sunderland

Isis CE Primary School, Oxford

Lancashire Primary Science Advisory Team

Llantilio Pertholey Primary School, Abergavenny

McLean Primary School, Dunfermline, Fife

Michael Rosen and the STAR* Project

Murton Primary School, Seaham, Co. Durham

Narinder Gill

St Thomas More RC Primary School, Durham

Thomas Swan and Co. Ltd, Consett, Co. Durham

Werrington Primary School, Cambridgeshire

Wold Primary School, Humberside

Yaxley Primary School, Cambridgeshire

My thanks also to Helen Johnson for her help and patience in editing this material and Colin Barker for coping with many changes to his page lay-outs.

Front cover photographs left to right: Wanda Parkes, Peter Ovens, Judith Manghan, Peter Ovens; *main cover photo,* copyright Ginn and Company, reproduced with permission.

Foreword

Science education for the year 2000 and beyond

The ASE document, *Science Education for the Year 2000 and Beyond*, states that:

Science is a distinct form of creative human activity which involves distinct ways of seeing, exploring and understanding reality. It is a fundamental part of everyday life and essential to our understanding of the world. It is a way of finding out about the world, requires imagination to create generalisations from laws, and to develop a growing body of ideas and information about the way things work. Science enables individuals to become curious and to seek explanations. As one of the essential features of any society, science has profound effects on people's lives and the environment, not least through its applications for practical purposes. It is an important part of every individual's education.

The Association believes that a child's experience of science should start as early as possible in the home, and then continue in nursery school. When children begin formal education science should be set within a broad, integrated curriculum within the primary curriculum. The Association believes that around 10 per cent of the time in the current primary curriculum should be spent on science.

The place of science in our lives is a dimension which encompasses a holistic view of science education. It will enable learners to:
* *participate fully in a technological society as informed citizens, who understand the nature of scientific ideas and activity and the basis for scientific claims; and*
* *develop intellectually and morally through experiencing the richness and excitement of exploring the natural and physical world.*

For individuals to participate as informed citizens in an ever-changing world, they require a sound science background and the skills of a literate person, so that they can access science and engage in dialogue.

Science has its own specific language to describe ideas, phenomena and ways of working, which allows scientists from different backgrounds, cultures and countries to communicate. Science is an international language, one to which the general public should have access so that we can understand and challenge the people who use it on our behalf, from governments to industry.

Many adults do not feel comfortable with science, or with information presented in a 'scientific' way. This is not simply a matter of public ignorance. If public understanding of science is to be developed, there needs to be a dialogue – a two-way communication – between those engaged in science and the public. (Feasey and Siraj-Blatchford, 1998)

Scientifiic knowledge is the product of a community, not an individual. Findings reported by an individual must survive an institutional checking and testing mechanism before being accepted as knowledge. (Driver *et al.*, 1996)

Not only should scientific knowledge have to survive institutional checking, but scientists must also be responsive to the concerns of the public who in turn should see it as their right and duty to challenge the scientific community.

The development of scientists and a scientifically literate population has its origins in the classroom where teachers expect pupils to explore their emerging scientific ideas and share ways of working with other people. For this to happen children need to develop a sound base of literacy skills which they can use to communicate how they think and work in science:

It is not easy to provide children with an accurate representation of scientific practice. However, by encouraging children to recognise the importance of the data they collect and to carefully consider how best to communicate their findings, investigations in the classrooms can mirror the activities of the science community. (Feasey and Siraj-Blatchford, 1998)

Children need to be confident in their use of language and their knowledge and understanding of science. Literate individuals have the tools with which to organise the ways they think and work in science as well as communicate their science to others using a range of approaches:

Pupils need to understand early ... that much of their writing will be read by others and, therefore, needs to be correct, legible and set out in appropriate and interesting ways. (The National Literacy Project Framework for Teaching, DfEE, 1998.)

All this depends on science in the primary school linking with literacy. The aim is for literacy skills to be used and developed in science, which offers a wide range of contexts, particularly those which are experiential and related to real-life situations. Equally important will be the use of science as a basis for Literacy Hours, offering contexts that are meaningful for children to learn and practise a range of skills, from writing continuous prose to creating poems based on a scientific observation or phenomenon. This partnership has enormous potential but teachers will have to ensure the integrity of the lesson: if the outcomes are literacy-based then science should be the vehicle; if science is the focus then literacy should be the servant, to help improve children's oral and written work.

Although the focus of this resource is literacy and the written word, the importance of the spoken word should not be underestimated. Children speak before they write, they frequently rehearse, rephrase and reorganise their ideas before committing them to paper or computer. The spoken word is central to literacy and science and should be afforded time in planning both literacy and science activities.

Conclusion

The world is truly awesome. A young child watching a beetle scuttling across a path is intrigued; a population of a country watching a solar eclipse is amazed. If we are comfortable with 'art for art's sake', we should be equally comfortable with the idea of 'science for science's sake', where individuals can participate in science-based activities simply because they enjoy them. An individual's access to 'science for science's sake' or for other more utilitarian reasons, has its base in personal literacy, from being able to access information in books and museums, to engaging in debate on genetic engineering on the Internet. All of this relies on someone's ability to read, write, comprehend and communicate – on this personal literacy.

Science benefits from a sound literacy base: equally literacy benefits from being used and developed in a whole range of interesting and challenging contexts within both formal and informal education. Scientifically literate individuals benefit the world in the discoveries they make, the inventions they use, the poetry they write and the science fiction that catapults us into other worlds and time zones, as well as offering access to the magic and beauty of the universe. Science and literacy are inextricably linked; our aim should be to help develop confident, articulate people who are able to engage in science at whatever level they choose.

References

ASE (1998) *Science Education for the Year 2000 and Beyond.* Hatfield, Herts: Association for Science Education.

DfEE (1998) *The National Literacy Srategy.* DfEE Publications.

Driver, R., Leach, J. and Scott, P. (1996) *Young people's images of science.* Buckingham: Open University Press.

Feasey, R. and Siraj-Blatchford, J. (1998) *Key skills: Communication in science.* Durham University and Tyneside TEC.

Using this resource

This resource is not intended to follow the National Literacy Strategy exactly, but to offer some ideas of how science and literacy can link successfully.

The material is organised into topic areas loosely linked to the National Literacy Strategy. Only a limited number of topics are covered; the aim is to stimulate links between science and literacy, rather than provide blanket coverage of the topics in the Literacy Strategy.

ARRANGEMENT OF THE TOPICS

The first part of this resource consists of four-page units each covering a topic area. Each unit has a similar lay-out.

FIRST PAGE

KEY ISSUES. Key points linked to the use and development in science of the aspect of the literacy document under consideration.

SUPPORTING STRATEGIES. A range of useful strategies to try with children to support work in the classroom.

SECOND PAGE

CHILDREN'S WORK. Examples of children's work, illustrating how the literacy skill can be applied and developed in science. The children's work also suggests different approaches and activities that can link literacy and science.

THIRD AND FOURTH PAGES

ACTIVITIES. Suggestions for either science-based lesson plans in which literacy links are highlighted and/or examples of a Literacy Hour where the literacy focus is placed in a science context. Where the focus is a science lesson it is important that the integrity of the science outcome is maintained and that the session does not become a literacy lesson. The principle is the same for Literacy Hours: although the context of the examples is science, the integrity of the literacy outcome must be maintained. Appropriate age levels are suggested.

PHOTOCOPIABLE RESOURCES

The second part consists of photocopiable resources for use in lessons, ranging from lists of scientific words and a framework for mini-books to poems and text which children can read and analyse.

ORAL RE-TELLING OF SCIENCE EXPERIENCES

KEY ISSUES

▶ Sharing ideas and describing activities orally helps children to organise their thoughts and reinforces learning.

▶ Explaining their science to other people helps children to make sense of their ideas.

▶ Being able to share their science with other people indicates to children that their work and ideas are valued.

▶ When children explain something orally they begin to organise and structure their ideas.

▶ Talking about a science activity or explaining ideas orally provides a useful rehearsal for writing about experiences.

▶ Sharing ideas and describing activities enables other people to ask questions and either reinforce or challenge what children are thinking and what they have done.

▶ The audience can take the role of 'critical friend', challenging children in a constructive way.

▶ Children need to be taught about the role of 'critical friend' and have experience of taking this role themselves.

SUPPORTING STRATEGIES

▶ Use circle time to offer opportunities for children to share and discuss ideas. Encourage children to ask each other questions to clarify points, seek additional information, and challenge what others have done or what they are thinking.

▶ Use questions to elicit information from children, help them sequence events and decide what information they should give others.

▶ Provide those children who need it with support and a structure to encourage them to make oral presentations.

▶ Help children to develop their ability to give oral presentations to a range of audiences by allowing them to practise in front of other children and receive constructive comments.

▶ Negotiate a 'Telling others about our science' framework with children. For example:
- *What were you trying to find out?*
- *What did you use and how did you do the activity?*
- *What were your results and what did you find out?*
- *What interesting things happened?*

Children's work

Children aged 6 and 7 visited the sea-shore and had the opportunity afterwards to re-tell their experiences:

'I collected eight shells. Each one was different from the others.'

'I was afraid there might be a crab hiding under the stones that was waiting to nip me.'

'When the tide came in the rock pool disappeared. It was covered with water.'

'There were hundreds of tiny baby mussels hiding in the little holes in the rocks.'

'Periwinkles are like snails. They come out of their shells when you hold them.'

GRANGE PARK PRIMARY SCHOOL, SUNDERLAND

Oral re-telling of science experiences

ACTIVITY 1A: Testing materials

SCIENCE LEARNING OUTCOMES

▶ **Understand that materials have different properties.**

▶ **Know that some materials are waterproof and some are not.**

▶ **Know that waterproof means that the material does not let water through.**

SCIENCE ACTIVITY

Teddy is going on a picnic but the weather forecast is not good. So Teddy needs a rainmac or an umbrella that will keep out water. What kind of material is waterproof and will keep Teddy dry?

This activity could be carried out with a small group where children suggest how they might test different materials. Offer children a range of resources as prompts, such as pipettes, syringes, yoghurt pots, fabrics and elastic bands. Ask them to think about what they could do, which pieces of equipment they could use and in what order they should do things. Create a simple table on which children can stick pieces of material to record their results:

Material	Did it let water through?

Allow the children to carry out their investigation and record their results. Talk with them about what happened and which material they would choose for Teddy's rainmac or umbrella. When the group has finished offer circle time for children to explain what they did to the rest of the class.

Very young children could carry out the testing by placing newspaper in the bottom of an empty water tray. The materials they are testing (in the form of umbrella panels) are placed over the paper and then tested using a small watering can. The successful umbrella panels will keep the newspaper underneath dry.

LITERACY LINK

During circle time allow children to tell others about their investigation. Give the group time beforehand to decide who will report on each part of the investigation. Children could be given prompts, such as a set of cards on each of which is written a different part of the investigation:

▶ **We got these things to use…**

▶ **This is what we did…**

▶ **This happened when we…**

▶ **This is how we recorded…**

Each child chooses a card and has to talk about that part of the investigation and perhaps offer a demonstration. The card prompts help the children to sequence what they are going to talk about. Each child has to place him or herself in the right order in relation to other people in the reporting group.

Oral re-telling of science experiences

ACTIVITY 1B: Pulse rates

SCIENCE LEARNING OUTCOMES

▶ Understand that exercise changes pulse rate.

▶ Know that generalisations can be made from data displayed in graphs which show patterns and trends.

SCIENCE ACTIVITY

Children plan and carry out an investigation to answer the question:

How does exercise affect pulse rate?

Each pair or group of children could investigate a different type of exercise. As part of their investigation tell the children that they will be expected to give a presentation to the rest of the class. During their presentation they have to explain how they carried out their investigation and discuss their results. They should expect the audience to ask questions.

Children may need practice in taking pulse rates before beginning the investigation.

⚠ **SAFETY.** Children with health problems, for example, asthma, should be recorders rather than exercisers.

LITERACY LINK

When they are preparing to give a presentation about their investigation, ask children to think about:

▶ who their audience is;

▶ what the audience needs to know;

▶ how they will present their information;

▶ the order in which the information should be given;

▶ the best way to present numerical data so that everyone can see the patterns and trends;

▶ how the presentation can be made interesting, for example, by the use of a demonstration or audience participation.

Encourage other children in the class to listen to the presentation and ask questions of the presenters.

TOPIC 2 ▶ LABELS AND CAPTIONS

KEY ISSUES

▶ Children should know that labels and captions are used to give a brief piece of information alongside a picture, diagram or model.

▶ Children should understand that labels and captions are a way of communicating information.

▶ Labels and captions are different. A *label* offers one or two words, telling you what something is. A *caption* can be a phrase or one or two sentences that help to explain something or add information.

▶ The teacher should tell children when they are using labels or captions so that children become familiar with and develop an understanding of both words.

▶ Children will need to be taught how to create labels and captions.

▶ Like all other written work, labels and captions should be written neatly or word-processed to ensure that they can be read easily.

▶ Children should be allowed to help the teacher make labels and captions for displays and to add to their own models and pictures.

▶ Children should be encouraged to draft and redraft their labels or captions.

SUPPORTING STRATEGIES

▶ Introduce labels by using Velcro stick-on labels that children can pull off and put on class wall displays or table-top activities, e.g. large flower or human body outline.

▶ Provide pre-cut cards of different sizes from which children can choose for labels and captions. This saves time and ensures that labels are neat and of a standard size.

▶ Allow children to work with an adult to scribe or word-process labels and captions.

▶ Create flags using cocktail sticks, plastic straws or lengths of dowelling. Use these for labels for three-dimensional work, e.g. models.

▶ Teach older children how to double-mount. This makes their labels and captions look more attractive and professional and helps them to appreciate how presentation can improve a finished product.

▶ The photocopiable resource on page 77 offers blank labels and caption boxes for children to use.

Children's work

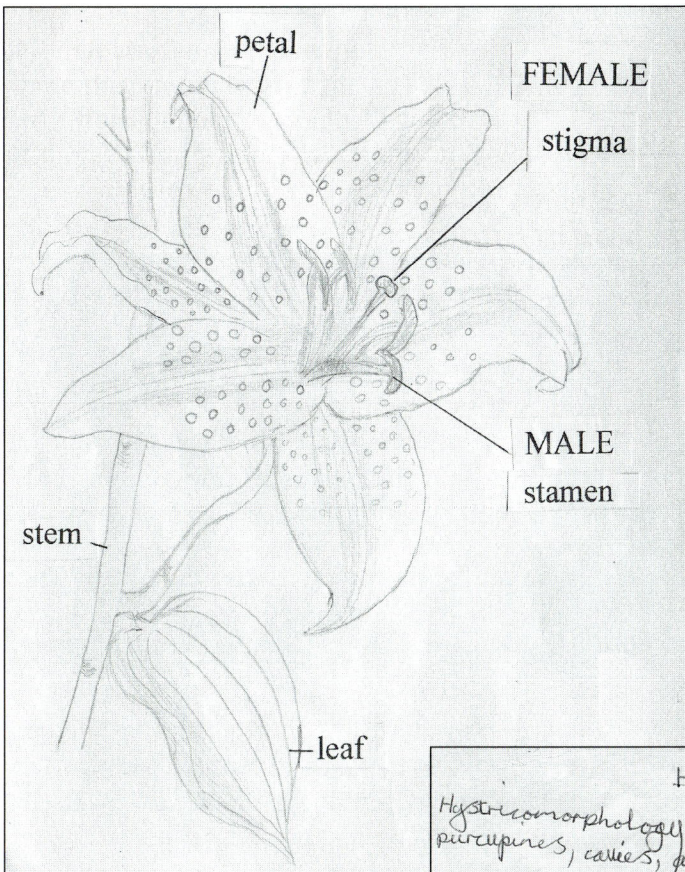

petal

FEMALE

stigma

MALE

stamen

stem

leaf

Y5, GRANGE PARK PRIMARY SCHOOL, SUNDERLAND

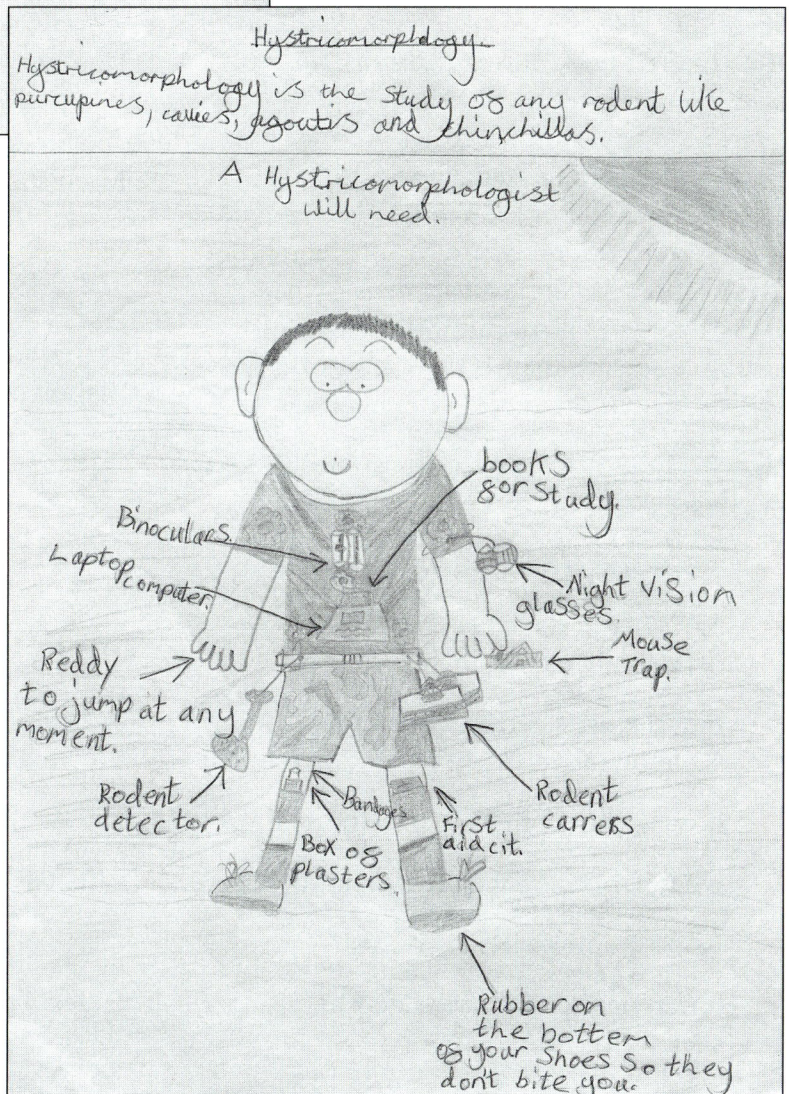

Children can learn about labels and captions in a range of contexts, from observing a flower to exploring scientific language by creating their own scientific terminology.

Hystricomorphology.

Hystricomorphology is the study of any rodent like porcupines, cavies, agoutis and chinchillas.

A Hystricomorphologist will need.

Binoculars.

Laptop computer.

books for study.

Night vision glasses.

Mouse Trap.

Reddy to jump at any moment.

Rodent detector.

Bandages.

Box of plasters.

First aid cit.

Rodent carress

Rubber on the bottem of your shoes so they don't bite you.

Y5, LLANTILIO PERTHOLEY PRIMARY SCHOOL, ABERGAVENNY

ACTIVITY 2A: Parts of the body

SCIENCE LEARNING OUTCOME

▶ Know the parts of the body.

SCIENCE ACTIVITY

A model skeleton always interests children and, although expensive for a school to purchase, model skeletons can be borrowed from a local secondary school or health authority. A life-size cardboard skeleton is usually within the budget of most primary schools.

LITERACY LINK

Read the Ahlbergs' book *Funny Bones* to the children and, during the story, discuss with them the different skeletons presented, e.g. human skeleton, dog, parrot, elephant and snake skeleton. Discuss with either the whole class or a small group of children what they already know about skeletons. Use their own experience to talk about the skeleton, for example feeling their own bones, or a visit to hospital with a broken bone.

Use the book to access science-based ideas such as:

▶ a skeleton is made up of bones;

▶ parts of the skeleton protect soft parts of the body, e.g. brain, heart, lungs;

▶ muscles are needed to make the skeleton move;

▶ how we know that we have bones;

▶ what happens if we break a bone;

▶ use of X-rays to look at bones;

▶ different animals have different skeletons.

Ask children to look at the model of a skeleton and name individual bones, e.g. skull, ribs, ankle bone. Show children different bones on the skeleton and ask them to find the corresponding bones in their own body.

In small groups, allow children access to a model or large picture of a skeleton. Ask them to either paint or create a model skeleton using Plasticine (the latter works if children create their skeleton horizontally on a base-board). Labels in the form of flags made from cocktail sticks or straws allow children to create labels for a Plasticine model. Depending on the children's language ability they could be asked to do one of the following:

▶ label their skeleton;

▶ write in the name of the bones on blank labels and place them on their skeleton;

▶ use prepared labels with the names of the bones already written on them and place them on the skeleton.

Display each of the skeletons created by the children and talk about:

▶ the different ways of labelling;

▶ the need for accuracy when they place a label next to a body part;

▶ the use of correct scientific words.

Labels and captions ▶ ACTIVITY 2B: Main body organs

SCIENCE LEARNING OUTCOMES

▶ Know the major organs of the body, e.g. heart, lungs, liver, kidneys.
▶ Know the function of each of the main organs of the body.

SCIENCE ACTIVITY

Give children an outline of a body or allow them to draw around each other. Challenge them to locate on the outline the major organs of the body and *label* them, and then to write *captions* explaining the function of the different organs in one or two phrases or sentences.

This activity helps to provide the teacher and children with evidence of what they already know about the position of organs in the body and about the function of each of the main organs.

LITERACY LINK

The aim of the second part of this activity is for children to research information about the different organs and then repeat the first activity, but this time positioning the organs accurately on the body and providing salient key points about each organ in a caption.

Children could research information about the major organs, such as:

▶ the position of the organ in the body;

▶ the size and shape of each organ;

▶ the main job of each organ;

▶ how it connects with other organs, e.g. heart and lungs.

This part of the activity could be organised as a whole-class, small-group, paired or individual activity, with children researching one or more of the organs. Where children are working in groups or a whole class, different children could be asked to research specific information to be shared with other children and incorporated in the captions.

Where one or more body outlines with labels and captions are created, invite children to compare the outlines and information. They should be encouraged to take the role of 'critical friend' and offer constructive criticism.

TOPIC 3 ▶ SCIENTIFIC VOCABULARY

KEY ISSUES

▶ Children need first-hand experience of scientific words, e.g. *transparent*, *force*, *habitat*, *dissolving*.

▶ The teacher should model correct scientific vocabulary in a range of appropriate contexts.

▶ Children should be challenged to use correct scientific words in their oral and written work.

▶ The teacher might need to help by scaffolding, using everyday and scientific terms in tandem (e.g. see-through and transparent), until children are confident in their use of the scientific term.

▶ Children need to understand that some everyday words have a specific meaning when used in a scientific context.

▶ Some words are incorrectly used by children to describe scientific phenomena. For example, children often say that something is 'melting' when they mean 'dissolving', as when a boiled sweet is sucked or when jelly cubes are placed in hot water.

▶ Children should be encouraged to have fun with science words, for example, crosswords and wordsearches. They could have access to some Latin names (e.g. plants) or make up their own scientific words.

SUPPORTING STRATEGIES

▶ **Word banks.** Create a bank of scientific terms related to each science topic. The words could be made available to children as a wall display, on a table top, in boxes or on special word bank sheets.

▶ **Word games.** Challenge children to create the longest list of scientific words related to a specific topic. Have a 'Guess my word' game, where children define or give clues to a scientific term for others to guess.

▶ **Concept maps.** Offer children key words to think about and with which to produce concept maps, in order to elicit language and assess their understanding of specific terms.

▶ **Mobiles.** Help children to create hanging word banks or mobiles, each displaying words under a specific heading, e.g. *friction*, *habitat*, *change*.

▶ Pages 78 and 79 provide a basic list of scientific vocabulary.

▶ Page 80 offers a vocabulary list related to the topic 'digestion'.

Looking at Fabrics

Piece Number	Woven or knitted or felt	Colour and shade	Texture	Pattern (draw)	How far can you stretch it?	What could it be used for?
	knitted	White	smooth softd		0 cm	it could be made into a Tshirt
	Woven	black and gold	bumpy		3cm	it could be made into a curtain
	woven	blue	bumpy		0 cm	it could be made into a cushion
	knitted	black	smooth		0 cm	it could be made into some trousers
	pressed	red	rough		2 cm	it could be made into a hat

Most children enjoy using scientific vocabulary. Children should have access to scientific words, both written and oral, and be challenged to think carefully about which words they should use to describe their ideas and experiences.

Y2, CUNNINGHAM HILL INFANT SCHOOL, ST ALBANS

Y1/2, YAXLEY PRIMARY SCHOOL, CAMBRIDGESHIRE

Science/English ~ Forces/Sentences

I can pull my cuborddatowards me,
I can squash my Playdough by
A force is a pull or a push.
I can push my bedroom door away pushing it.
When I stetch some tithes they from me.
becuse am pulling them. get longer
I can push a trolley
I can pull a door towards me.

Scientific vocabulary ▶ ACTIVITY 3A: Exploring forces

SCIENCE LEARNING OUTCOMES

▶ Understand the use of the word *fair* in a scientific context and use it appropriately.

▶ Understand the meaning of a *pull* force.

SCIENCE ACTIVITY

A 'tug-of-war' is a good way of exploring forces. Set up unfair competitions, such as two children against one or the tallest against the smallest, and ask the children if they think it is fair. Then ask what they think fair means and how they would make the tug-of-war fair.

Encourage the children to talk about the forces in action during the tug-of-war and to use words associated with forces.

Photographs of different children in 'fair' and 'unfair' tugs-of-war could be used as a focal point for discussion about forces.

LITERACY LINK–LITERACY HOUR

The Literacy Hour can focus on **guided writing** with children using a range of scientific language, such as *fair* and *unfair*, *push*, *pull*, *balanced*, *unbalanced*, *friction*, *slide*, *grip*, *stick*, *slip*. Model these words and expect children to use them when they are describing or explaining what is happening in the activity.

SHARED TEXT WORK (15 MINS)

Children could be offered a series of sentences to read which use the above words, and then mime the actions.

FOCUSED WORD AND SENTENCE WORK (15 MINS)

Create a tug-of-war book containing the photographs from the activity. Ask children to explain what is happening in the photograph in which they feature and to write a commentary for it. They should use the scientific words on the class display to explain whether the tug-of-war in their photograph was a fair or unfair test and what forces were acting.

INDEPENDENT WRITING (20 MINS)

Use a large display of a tug-of-war with life-size paintings of children pulling each end of a rope. Ask children to think about sentences (captions) to go on the display, using the words displayed around the picture. To encourage and help children to use the range of words produce a word bank. Children who have difficulty creating sentences can construct their sentence using the word bank (perhaps words on cards) and copy or word-process the sentence.

Merely making a word bank available will not ensure that children use it. They need to be provided with structure and support, including close 'interference' in their work, to ensure quality of experience.

WHOLE-CLASS REVIEW (10 MINS)

Ask children to read out their own captions which can then be discussed in terms of the use of correct scientific words.

Scientific vocabulary ▶ Activity 3B: Plants make their own food

Science learning outcome

▶ Understand that plants make their own food.

Science activity

Ask children to draw a plant, for example a sunflower, and to annotate the plant to explain:

▶ **what plants need to live;**

▶ **where they get their water from;**

▶ **where they get their food from.**

Let children share their ideas; they could be placed around a large sunflower drawn on an OHP or a chalkboard. Ask children to consider whether or not they agree with an idea. Where they disagree, ask them to offer evidence or reasons why they think that idea is probably wrong. For example, some children might think that plants in a pot get their food from the soil. If this were so, logic would suggest that the soil would disappear or at least it would weigh less as the plant got bigger.

Give children access to a range of books or material on photosynthesis and encourage them to try to understand the process by which plants make their own food. Explain the process within the class. Using a whole-class lesson or small groups challenge children to work towards a consensus in their thinking about how plants get their food. Although the explanation at this level is relatively simple the word *photosynthesis* can be introduced because explaining the word can help children to remember the process. Explain that the prefix *photo* means light and that *synthesis* means putting smaller parts together to make something bigger.

Literacy link–Literacy Hour

This Literacy Hour activity focuses on **prefixes**. It uses the photocopiable material on page 81.

Shared text work (15 mins)
Discuss with children the use of prefixes in their written work, for example, *in, il, im, un,* and how these change the base-word into a negative. Offer the children text containing examples of prefixes and ask them to identify the words and the prefix. Talk about what the words would mean if the prefix was taken away.

Introduce children to the idea that there is a range of prefixes, and that each one has its own meaning which can give a clue to the meaning of a word or group of words. Discuss examples such as: *aero* (air), *bio* (life). Ask children to think about words beginning with these prefixes, for example *aeroplane, aerodynamic, aerosol, biology, biodiversity, biotechnology.* Challenge them to take clues from the prefix and the rest of the word to suggest what the words might mean.

Focused word and sentence work (15 mins)
Give children a copy of page 81 on prefixes and ask them to work through the task of creating their own definitions of the words. This could be done as a class discussion or with children drafting their own definitions. Do not allow access to dictionaries at this point; children must take clues from the prefixes and words themselves.

Independent writing (20 mins)
In this session children check their own definitions with those offered by dictionaries. Children write down the dictionary definition and give their own attempt a score out of 10. Ask children to think of other prefixes and words that include them, and make their own list or table.

Whole-class review (10 mins)
Discuss the different prefixes and words, encouraging children to extend the examples on the photocopied page.

TOPIC 4 ▶ DICTIONARIES AND GLOSSARIES

KEY ISSUES

▶ Dictionaries and glossaries are different: a *dictionary* provides definitions of a wide range of words whilst a *glossary* only defines words in a particular book.

▶ Children should be encouraged to explore a wide range of scientific terms.

▶ Children should experience science dictionaries and glossaries in non-fiction science books.

▶ Children need experience of using a dictionary and a glossary before making their own.

▶ Creating their own science dictionaries and glossaries helps children to understand their nature and purpose.

▶ Creating a science dictionary or a glossary helps to indicate and develop children's understanding of specific scientific terms.

▶ Children should draft and redraft their definitions.

▶ The teacher should encourage children to try out their definitions on other children or adults as they draft them.

▶ Developing individual, group or class definitions of words in science provides a useful means of assessing children's understanding of science concepts.

▶ Dictionaries and glossaries can be interactive. For instance, a dictionary of materials could include samples for children to feel, look at and examine closely.

▶ It is important to make sure that dictionaries and glossaries are used regularly in science work.

SUPPORTING STRATEGIES

▶ Offer a range of examples of different dictionaries and glossaries, especially those that use scientific terms.

▶ Discuss with children the purpose and format of a dictionary or glossary.

▶ In early years the teacher could create a simple dictionary or glossary with the class as a class book.

▶ Allow children to work with a friend or in a small group when developing their definitions of words.

▶ Limit the number of words that children have to define in early years and increase the number as children get older and more experienced.

▶ Where children create a dictionary the following is often a useful framework to support them in defining a word:
- *What does the word mean?*
- *Give an example of the word in real life.*
- *Use the word to talk about something you have seen or done.*

▶ At the beginning or end of sessions challenge children to offer definitions of words used during a lesson. Ask them to check their definition against their own or a published science dictionary or glossary.

▶ Pages 82 and 83 provide frameworks for dictionary and glossary work.

Children's work

Children created a dictionary where they not only offered definitions but also placed examples of materials and objects on each page.

flexible

If something is flexible you can bend it easily without breaking it.

A pipe-cleaner is flexible.

Hair, paper and wool are flexible too.

Y3, COPTHORNE FIRST SCHOOL, BRADFORD

Where children develop dictionaries and glossaries they should be challenged to draft and redraft definitions.

A-Z of the Body

Atria
Brain
Cranida
Dermis
Epidermis
Fibula
Gland
Heart
Intestine
Jaw
Knee
Liver
Marrow

Nerve
Organs
Phalanges
Quit
Rectum
Scapula
Tibia
Ulna
Ventricle
Wrist
X-ray
Yawn
Zit

MERIT

Y4, ISIS CE PRIMARY SCHOOL, OXFORD

ACTIVITY 4A: Plant growth

SCIENCE LEARNING OUTCOMES

▶ Know the different parts of a plant.

▶ Know the functions of the different parts of a plant.

▶ Understand what plants need to live.

SCIENCE ACTIVITY

Give children a set of bean plants (or pictures of bean plants) at different stages of growth: seed, germinating seed, root and shoot growing, first leaves, established plant. Ask them to observe and compare the different stages of plant growth and discuss the features of the fully grown plant. Are all the features on all of the plants, e.g. leaves, flowers, root hairs?

Children can identify and discuss the different parts of a plant, such as *root, stem, stalk, leaf, flower, petal, root hairs, seed* and *seed case*. Encourage them to discuss what each part does and relate this to what they know about life processes. Let children observe the root hairs on one of the plants using a hand lens.

Give the children labels to match to different parts of the fully grown plant. Let them choose a caption and match it to a part of the plant; they can then describe that part of the plant and what it does.

LITERACY LINK–LITERACY HOUR

This set of activities can be carried out in a Literacy Hour, the aim being for each child to produce a **mini-dictionary** of between 6 and 12 words depending on their age and ability. The mini-dictionary is an A4 sheet of paper folded into a small book.

SHARED TEXT WORK (15 MINS)
Get children to read extracts from a dictionary appropriate to their age and ability. Discuss with them the format of a dictionary and alphabetical order.

FOCUSED WORD AND SENTENCE WORK (15 MINS)
Give children a small selection of words related to the topic of plants. Ask them to put these in alphabetical order and then draft a simple explanation of the word. For example, *root, stem, leaf, flower, root hairs.*

INDEPENDENT WRITING (20 MINS)
Now ask children to use their words and definitions to create their own dictionary. Each page, in alphabetical order, should have a letter at the top, with the word and definition written underneath.

WHOLE-CLASS REVIEW (10 MINS)
The children share their dictionaries and talk about the words they have defined. It is useful if the children have different words.

Dictionaries and glossaries ACTIVITY 4B: Properties of materials

SCIENCE LEARNING OUTCOMES

▶ Know properties of materials.

▶ Understand that materials are chosen for everyday uses because of their properties.

▶ Use correct scientific terms when discussing properties of materials.

SCIENCE ACTIVITY

Give children a selection of words describing properties of materials to define. Then give them a range of materials to test to find out which property or properties they possess. For example, *waterproof, rigid, flexible, transparent.*

Create a simple table for children to complete:

Property	Materials	Everyday uses

Work from this activity will contribute towards a class glossary on the properties of materials.

LITERACY LINK–LITERACY HOUR

SHARED TEXT WORK (15 MINS)

Read examples of glossaries with the children and discuss key features.

FOCUSED WORD AND SENTENCE WORK (15 MINS)

Let children look up and read definitions of a range of scientific words related to the properties of materials, such as *absorbent, flexible, rigid, transparent,* and write down a definition. Then ask children to draft their own definitions of the scientific words to a set format which will form part of a whole-class glossary.

INDEPENDENT WRITING (20 MINS)

Children can now develop their scientific word work and illustrate that they understand the definitions by providing examples of materials with particular properties and everyday contexts in which they are used. Ask them to write down an example of an everyday object made from a material with a particular property. Encourage them to think of other examples of materials and objects made from them which have the same property.

WHOLE-CLASS REVIEW (10 MINS)

The children share their definitions and challenge the wording of definitions where appropriate. Encourage them to suggest alternative examples of the properties in everyday contexts that could also be used in their glossary.

TOPIC 5 ▶ SEQUENCING EVENTS

KEY ISSUES

▶ Sequencing events helps children to order their ideas.

▶ Sequencing events helps children to develop a logical approach to thinking and working in science.

▶ Children can be helped in remembering what happened, by prompting:
  • *What happened next?*
  • *Then what did you do?*

▶ Challenging children to sequence in science is a good way of providing a framework and model for investigations. A planning framework which clearly leads children through a sequence of thinking can then support them in carrying out an activity.

▶ Asking children to sequence events challenges them to decide what are the most important events or what their ideas are. It can help them to think about what they should leave out as well as what they must keep.

▶ There are many different approaches to sequencing in science, from using photographs and pictures to asking children to create flow diagrams, circle diagrams or instructions.

SUPPORTING STRATEGIES

▶ Introduce children to ways of recording that help them to sequence events, such as strip-cartoons, flow diagrams and circle diagrams (e.g. life cycles).

▶ Discuss the event or their planning and ask children to answer questions such as:
  • *What happened next?*
  • *What are you going to do or think about next?*

▶ Ask children to sequence cards on which an activity is described in words or pictures. If the sequence is about an investigation or other practical activity, the cards could then be used to support children in carrying out the activity.

▶ Use 'planning houses', 'planning boards' or similar frameworks to help children to share ideas about what they are going to do or have done. These are excellent for supporting children in sequencing ideas and activities.

▶ Take a set of photographs of an activity and use them to sequence events and explain scientific ideas. The photocopiable page 76 offers an opportunity to sequence events and talk about forces.

▶ Show children how to make folding mini-books which they can use to sequence their explanation of how they carried out an investigation. A template for a folding mini-book is given on pages 85 and 86.

Children's work

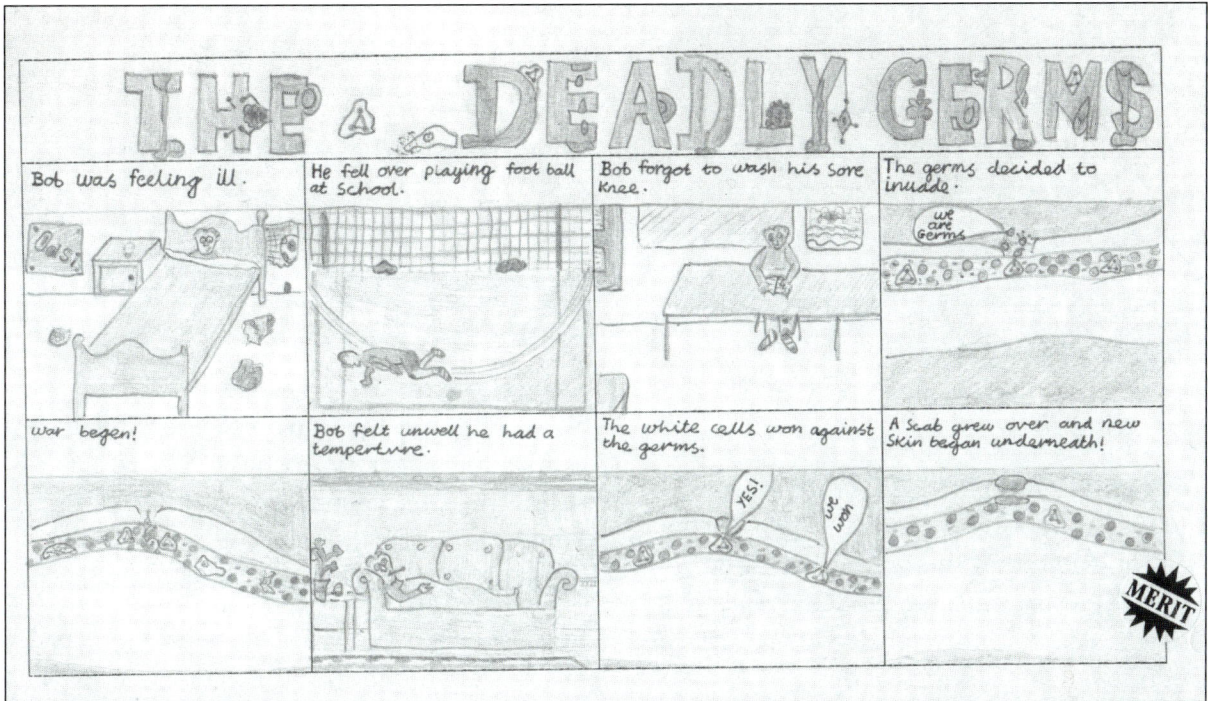

THE DEADLY GERMS

Bob was feeling ill.

He fell over playing football at school.

Bob forgot to wash his sore knee.

The germs decided to invade.

we are germs

war began!

Bob felt unwell he had a temperture.

The white cells won against the germs.

A scab grew over and new skin began underneath!

YES!

we won

MERIT

Y4, ISIS CE PRIMARY SCHOOL, OXFORD

Offering children different methods of sequencing events can help them develop the ability to order their ideas, knowledge and experiences.

September 19th 97   Amy Green

<u>My Adventure</u>

Milly Mango was having a nice chat with Katie Kiwi, Percy Pear and Adam Apple, When suddenly her friends started to disappear.
"Whats happening?" she said to herself. But as she said it, she got lifted off her feet.
"Ahh!" she yelled, as she flew into the air.
"Oww!" she yelled again.
Milly Mango looked down. As she looked down she realized she had no legs. Then all my body suddenly I felt myself slip down a long tube (epiglotus). Then I landed, plop into a large, dark and wet room.
"Percy! is that you", shouted Milly crushed Mango.
"Yes!" shouted Percy crushed pear.
"Where are we?" asked Milly.
Percy answered,
"We have just been past the oesophegus and have fallen in the stomach."
"So you mean were in the body's digestive system?" said Milly.
"Whoa!" Milly screamed, as she was pushed along by a wave. Milly found herself in the rectum with all her friends. The a few hours later she found her self in light Lobbing in water.
She realized she was in the toilet

Good Amy – but you missed out the intestines, appendix –––

Y5/6, GRANGE PARK PRIMARY SCHOOL, SUNDERLAND

R/Y1

Sequencing events

ACTIVITY 5A: Cooking eggs

SCIENCE LEARNING OUTCOMES

▶ Understand that materials can change when heated.

▶ Know that some materials cannot be changed back to the way they were before they were heated (not reversible).

SCIENCE ACTIVITY

Divide children into groups to make scrambled eggs.

Give children the set of pictures of the recipe for making scrambled eggs on page 84. Tell them that the recipe has been jumbled up by mistake and that they will have to put it in the right order before they begin to make scrambled eggs.

Discuss with children why they chose that order and what kind of changes they think will take place when they make the scrambled eggs.

Using the pictures, ask children to tell you (or the adult working them) what they have to do to make the scrambled eggs. At each stage ask children to think about what will happen next and what they think caused the change. Use specific vocabulary, such as *runny, change, mix, heat, pour, stir.*

Let children eat the scrambled eggs and compare them with the whole eggs they started out with. They will probably need an egg in a shell and an egg out of its shell in a bowl for immediate comparison.

The following activity could be carried out in the Literacy Hour. (A digital camera could be used to take photographs of children making the scrambled eggs and used to create the zig-zag book and sentences.)

LITERACY LINK–LITERACY HOUR

SHARED TEXT WORK (15 MINS)

Show children an example of a zig-zag book (an extra large version so that all children can see) and discuss the contents, which might be 'the story of scrambled eggs' using photographs and sentences.

FOCUSED WORD AND SENTENCE WORK (15 MINS)

Discuss with children the construction of sentences explaining the process of making scrambled eggs using the photocopied pictures or the photographs as prompts. Ask children to place the pictures in the correct order. Scribe their sentences on to a board and negotiate sentence construction before placing each sentence under the correct picture. Challenge children to be critical of each sentence and make sure that the sequence is correct.

INDEPENDENT WRITING (20 MINS)

Ask children to tell the story of how to make scrambled eggs, making sure that what they write is in the correct sequence. Depending on the ability of the children they could be asked to complete 4, 6 or 8 sections in a zig-zag book. Some children will require a scribe; others could attempt to write their own sentences, with or without the material to support sentence construction.

WHOLE-CLASS REVIEW (10 MINS)

Ask children to read out their own story and discuss the sequence and detail of each story. Encourage children to describe what happened and why they think it happened; for example, *the heat made the eggs change.*

Sequencing events

ACTIVITY 5B: DIGESTIVE SYSTEM

SCIENCE LEARNING OUTCOMES

▶ Know the names of parts of the digestive system.

▶ Be able to describe the main stages of digestion of food.

SCIENCE ACTIVITY

The starting point for this lesson could be children eating a piece of food, chewing it and mixing it with saliva, and thinking about what happens to it as it passes through the digestive system. As children are eating elicit their understanding of the digestive process. Ask them to draw on an outline of the body what they think happens to food after it is put in the mouth. Discuss children's ideas and the evidence they have for them.

Follow up by offering children the opportunity to research the digestive system using science non-fiction books, CD-ROMs, posters and models. Ask them to make notes on the key points and then use their notes to improve their original drawings of the digestive system.

LITERACY LINK

Children can use the information they have researched and recorded on digestion to produce a flow diagram as an *aide-mémoire* to explain digestion in the correct sequence and using correct scientific terminology. Allow children to swap flow diagrams and check each other's work. Ask them to write comments on the work relating to:

correct sequence;

accuracy;

use of scientific terms.

Once the children are confident with their own understanding of the digestive system, ask them to use information from their notes and flow diagram to help them to write a story about the journey of a piece of food. They should tell the story from eating the food to elimination of waste.

The story could be written as if the child is the piece of food journeying through the digestive system. Children should be challenged to:

ensure that the sequence of events is correct;

identify the tense to be used;

check that their scientific information is correct;

use scientific words where appropriate.

Page 80 offers a vocabulary list linked to this activity.

TOPIC 6 ▶ USING TENSES, VERBS, ADJECTIVES, ETC.

KEY ISSUES

▶ The correct use of tenses is important when children talk and write about science.

▶ Children need to talk and write in present tense. For example:
I am thinking about ...

▶ In their planning, children need to talk and write in future tense. For example:
We will, We should, We are going to.

▶ In describing what they have done children need to talk or write in the past tense. For example:
We did this, When we got, Then, When we did that this happened.

▶ It is important that the teacher models the different tenses when he or she talks to children as well as offering a written model.

▶ The teacher should draw children's attention to the fact that they are writing about something that has happened or is going to happen, that is past or future tense.

▶ Children should be given the opportunity to talk through their ideas before they write so that they can rehearse the construction of sentences.

▶ Children's work should be corrected in relation to the tenses used and errors discussed with them.

SUPPORTING STRATEGIES

▶ Use scaffolding when necessary to help children use future tense, through writing and speaking frameworks, such as planning frameworks for investigations.

▶ Use scaffolding when necessary to help children use past tense, through writing and speaking frameworks, such as reporting frameworks which offer a series of questions or suggested headings.

▶ Page 87 offers a photocopiable piece of children's writing in science. Children can be given copies and asked to highlight verbs, different tenses and adjectives.

▶ Ask children to write their own stories using a science context. This provides them with opportunities to develop their ability to use tenses, verbs, etc., correctly.

▶ Use circle time to talk through what children are planning to do or what they have done. Help children to reconstruct sentences to ensure that they have used tenses correctly.

▶ Offer children a set of openers or connective words or phrases to help them write and talk about science. For example:
When we, After that we, We found out, This happened.

Using tenses, verbs, adjectives, etc.

Children's work

Children's work should be checked for the use of correct tense when writing in science. Before children begin writing rehearse orally what they will write and which tense they will use.

Shadows

We made a man with multilink. We got a bit of paper. We put the man by the paper. The torch was 172 cms away. We put the man near the paper and the shadow was big. We drew rownd the man when he was big and when he was small and near the paper we drew rownd the shadow. We used a torch for the sun. We used a meter stick. We used ruler with cms. We wanted to find out about shadows. In summer the sun is directly sineing on the man in winnter the sun is not directly on the man. We put the torch in different places and got different shadows. We wrote on a bit of paper how far away the torch was from the man. We got 172.5 ms, 20 cms. 118cms, 114cm. When the man was 20 cms away from the paper the shadow was small. when we put it 118 away it was big.

Practical investigation with partner to see how shadows change. Linked to seasons topic.
20 Jan 98

Y2, CUNNINGHAM HILL INFANT SCHOOL, ST ALBANS

ACTIVITY 6A: Forces

SCIENCE LEARNING OUTCOMES

Understand that a force is a *push* or a *pull*.

Know that a force can make something start to move.

Appreciate that the bigger the push or pull force the further something moves.

SCIENCE ACTIVITY

Read the book *Mr Gumpy's Motor Car* by John Burningham to the children and discuss it. Talk to children about what the animals had to do to get the car out of the mud. Encourage them to use correct scientific vocabulary, such as *push, pull, force.*

Discuss with the children what affects how easy or how hard it is to move something, for example:

Is it the surface?

Is it how heavy something is?

Is it to do with how big something is?

Is it whether it has wheels?

Discuss with children the question:

Which is the best surface for Mr Gumpy's car to move over?

Help children to plan, using a planning house or other type of framework, and carry out an investigation to answer the question. Children could use carpet, wood or any other kind of surface over which to make a car move. Discuss the idea of a fair test and how they will know which surface is the best. Will it be the one that allows the car to travel the furthest?

Encourage children to record their results as a table and then to represent the information as a bar chart.

LITERACY LINK—LITERACY HOUR

SHARED TEXT WORK (15 MINS)
Ask the children to read a passage from the book which uses tenses, verbs or adjectives and discuss the use of words with them. Ask them to re-read it, picking out words that are in the past tense or words that are adjectives or verbs.

FOCUSED WORD AND SENTENCE WORK (15 MINS)
Give each child a list of verbs and ask them to change the tense by adding *ed.* Alternatively they could produce their own list of verbs by extracting them from a passage they have read.

INDEPENDENT WRITING (20 MINS)
Give each child a series of pictures, which could be based on the book, or a set of cartoon-type action pictures showing someone *pushing, pulling, squashing, hitting, twisting, stretching.* Ask the children to write a sentence underneath each one using past tense; for example, '*The elephant squashed the tomato*'. Where appropriate offer children a word bank to support them in writing their sentences and choosing the correct word.

WHOLE-CLASS REVIEW (10 MINS)
Discuss the pictures with the children and ask them to read out their sentences. Offer alternative pictures for discussion. Get children to mime actions that other children have to describe in sentences using past tense: '*John pressed his hands together.*'

Using tenses, verbs, adjectives, etc.

ACTIVITY 6B: Dissolving

SCIENCE LEARNING OUTCOME

▶ Know that some materials dissolve and others do not.

SCIENCE ACTIVITY

Provide children with experience of materials that do and do not dissolve in water; for example, *sand, salt, jelly crystals, coffee granules, flour, Marmite, granulated sugar*. Ask them to find out which materials dissolve in water and to record their results in a table. Discuss the results with the children.

Then ask children to take four of the materials that do dissolve and answer the question:

Which material dissolves the fastest?

Children should offer a detailed plan before they begin the investigation. Talk to the children about what they should include in their plan, such as:

▶ equipment;

▶ who will carry out which job;

▶ what they will do;

▶ what they will measure;

▶ how they will record;

▶ how they will keep it fair;

▶ in what order they will do things.

Discuss their plans with the children before allowing them to carry out their investigation.

LITERACY LINK

The planning of the investigation enables the teacher to focus children's attention on the use of future tense, such as:

▶ we will;

▶ we are going to;

▶ the next thing we will do is;

▶ after that we shall.

Children might need support when planning, to ensure that they use the correct words and phrases. Page 88 offers suggestions for openers and connectives that include future tense and can be used as mobiles to hang around the classroom, as phrases on display boards or individual table-top phrase banks for children to use.

TOPIC 7 ▶ USING OPENERS AND CONNECTIVES

KEY ISSUES

▶ Children often find it difficult to express themselves when writing in science.

▶ Openers and connectives are words and phrases that help children to begin sentences or link parts of a sentence together.

▶ Openers and connectives can be used as prompts to suggest what to write and which aspects of an investigation should be included.

▶ As with all language, children need to experience openers and connectives modelled by someone else.

▶ The teacher should model the use of openers and connectives in his or her speech and writing in science.

▶ The teacher should also make it explicit when openers and connectives are being used so that children can recognise them.

SUPPORTING STRATEGIES

▶ Create a bank of openers and connectives for children to use and display them around the classroom.

▶ Have class sessions where, having carried out the same activity, the whole class negotiates what to write using a series of connectives. The teacher acts as scribe, writing on a board or OHP what the children agree.

▶ Before children write up their science, decide as a class which openers and connectives could be used and challenge children to use them in their writing.

▶ In oral feedback challenge children to use openers and connectives in their speech. For example:

Using our results we noticed that ....

▶ Page 88 offers photocopiable material with connectives and openers in speech bubbles.

Children's work

Children need to be taught a range of openers and connectives and offered opportunities to use them. In this example a writing frame offers a series of openers.

My Investigation it is about shadows

I want to find out if the Shadows gow little ones bigger when the torch moves

I did this we used the torch and we made a multilink man shadow

I found out I that wen we put the torch closer the shadow go's big. win we put the torch further away it made the shadow smaller.

Y2, CUNNINGHAM HILL INFANT SCHOOL, ST ALBANS

As children become more confident, the support of writing frames should gradually be taken away so that they become more independent in their writing.

The red group were deciding how to keep the sound out of our ears. Then an idea came into our heads. One person stood behind a ruler and one person stood behind another ruler. Katie stood behind one ruler with a triangle in her hand. I had cotton wool to block my ears. I tried to hear the sounds. If I could I said yes and if I couldn't I said no. I thought that cotton was the best material to block the sound out of your ears.

Y2, CILFFRIW PRIMARY SCHOOL, NEATH

Openers such as 'The red group were deciding' and 'I thought that' help children to construct descriptions of their investigations which flow.

Materials used in houses

Some materials used in houses are Plastic wood bricks and glass. You use all of these materials because you would not have any where to live if you did not have materials. You use wood to make window frames, you use bricks to make walls. When you use glass you make windows.

Y2/3, CALTON JUNIOR SCHOOL, GLOUCESTER

ACTIVITY 7A: Shadows

SCIENCE LEARNING OUTCOMES

▶ Know that shadows are caused when light is blocked.

▶ Know that the size of a shadow can be changed.

SCIENCE ACTIVITY

This activity is most successful when carried out using a strong light source. The best light source is an OHP, but it is important to ensure that the projector is secure and cannot be knocked or pulled over. Alternatively a strong torch or slide projector could be used; ensure that the latter is safe for children to use. This activity should be part of exploring shadows, for example:

▶ How are shadows made?

▶ Which materials make the best shadows?

▶ What do we have to do to change a shadow?

Ask the children to find out what they have to do to change the size of a shadow. They could use an object such as a teddy bear and explore how to make it bigger and smaller. When the children understand how to change the size of a shadow, encourage them to look for a pattern in the distance of Teddy from the light and the size of his shadow. Give them a simple table to complete:

How far Teddy is from the light	Size of the shadow

Discuss the results with the children. Talk about the link between the distance from the light source and the size of Teddy's shadow. Ask them to complete a set of sentences, such as:

If you want Teddy's shadow to be about 40 centimetres you have to put Teddy .... centimetres from the light.

LITERACY LINK

Writing in science can be difficult for many children. Offering a set of opening statements to provide clues about what to write provides positive support. Children could be offered some or all of the following openers:

▶ Before you make a shadow you have to...

▶ Then what you have to do is...

▶ After that you...

▶ If you want to make the shadow bigger...

▶ We looked at our results and they told us that...

▶ We found out that .... you have to...

This set of openers provides children with a framework for writing and also models the use of words associated with time such as *before, then, after*. Alternatively, a different set appropriate to the ability and needs of the children could be developed. However, writing frames should only be seen as initial support; gradually children should become independent of them.

Using openers and connectives › ## ACTIVITY 7B: Dissolving

SCIENCE LEARNING OUTCOME

▶ Know that some materials dissolve in a liquid.

SCIENCE ACTIVITY

Ask children what they know about dissolving. Brainstorm ideas by asking questions such as:

▶ **What does it mean when something has dissolved?**

▶ **How would you know when something has dissolved?**

Keep a record of their suggestions to compare with their ideas later in the topic. Encourage them to discuss ideas, accepting some and discarding others, until they reach an agreed list of criteria. They might decide that dissolving is when:

▶ **a solid material mixes with a liquid;**

▶ **a solid material stays mixed with a liquid;**

▶ **the liquid is clear.**

Give children a range of solids to try to dissolve in water and ask them to record the results. This could be in the form of a table:

Solid	Stays mixed	Clear	Dissolved

LITERACY LINK

When children have completed the activity ask them to write a short account of it, using a simple writing frame. Discuss the idea of using openers to help them to decide what to write. Children should include a description of what they did, tell the reader what happened, and justify how they know that some things dissolve and others do not.

▶ **We were trying to find out...**

▶ **When we put ... into it...**

▶ **I know it dissolved because...**

▶ **However the ... did not dissolve because...**

▶ **We can tell when things dissolve because...**

Ask children to read their accounts to each other and talk about how the writing frame helps them to explain what they have been doing and their results. When children have completed all of the activity return to their original ideas about dissolving and ask them to think about whether they have changed. Ask if they want to remove any of their original statements and what they could write in their place. More openers and connectives can be found on page 88.

TOPIC 8 ▶ ASKING QUESTIONS

KEY ISSUES

▶ Questioning is a linguistic form. Children need to be taught the structure of a question.

▶ Children need to see and hear the teacher and other adults working with them modelling effective questions.

▶ The teacher should check that he or she is offering children a wide set of question stems, such as:

What?, Where?, When?, Why?, How?, If?, What if?, Could?, Should?

▶ An effective scientific question is one that has a definite science outcome.

▶ Children should be taught the difference between an open and a closed question.

▶ Children should be offered many opportunities to ask their own questions as a whole class, as groups and individually.

▶ The classroom should be full of opportunities for children to see, ask and answer questions. Questions should be modelled as part of classroom displays, on question boards and as part of the everyday talk in the classroom.

▶ Children's questions should be valued. They should feel confident that their questions will be accepted and that at some point opportunities will be given for their questions to be answered.

SUPPORTING STRATEGIES

▶ Brainstorm questions with children so that they can learn from each other about different types of questions.

▶ Brainstorm with children question stems such as *When?, What?* and *Who?*, and challenge them to keep adding to the list and to use question stems in their own work.

▶ Use questions on displays to attract attention, draw children into a display and to make a display interactive.

▶ Display children's questions to show that the questions are valued.

▶ Create question mobiles. Hang questions from the ceiling.

▶ Create a question board on which children can post their own questions.

▶ Make a post box in which children can post their own questions. Empty the post box regularly and share the questions with the class.

▶ Challenge children to ask a certain number of questions or to ask enough questions on a topic to go right round the room, the corridor or the school.

▶ Create class question books where children can add their own questions over time or collect questions on certain topics.

▶ Page 89 offers a photocopiable framework for asking questions, with examples of question stems.

Children's work

friuts

① What is it called? it is called a satsuma

② is it cold? yes it is cold

③ what size is it? it is 20cm around the middle

④ what shape is it? it is a sphere/safer shape

⑤ has it got seeds? yes it has got seeds

⑥ what colour is it? the colour is orange

⑦ has it got spikes? no it has'not

⑧ does it have a storh? yes it does

⑨ if you drop it will it smace? no it won't

⑩ what does it smell like? it smells like a flower

⑪ does it spin? yes it does spin   `18 NOV 1997`

⑫ what does it look like? it looks like an orange
But it's smaller.   When you rush you forget
'sentences' Capitals, full stops!

To ensure that children produce quality written work in science the teacher must remind children that aspects of language such as full stops and capital letters are important.

Y2, CUNNINGHAM HILL INFANT SCHOOL, ST ALBANS

Key Stage 1

My Question.....

which car is the best

I will change.....

the car

I will make it fair.....

we didn't push it
we used a rular
we rolled the cars on the slope

I predict that.....

I think my car is the best
because... my car is a raceingcar

I found out that.....

robin was the best

Questions are central to science: they should be a permanent feature of the classroom.

Y2, SUE DICKENSON, LANCASHIRE PRIMARY SCIENCE ADVISORY TEAM

Y2

Asking questions ▶ ACTIVITY 8A: Fruit and vegetables

SCIENCE LEARNING OUTCOMES

▶ Develop questioning skills through observation.

▶ Understand how to use all of the senses to explore objects.

▶ Know that a fruit holds the seeds of a plant.

SCIENCE ACTIVITY

Offer children a range of fruit and vegetables to explore using all their senses. Give each child a fruit or a vegetable and allow them to observe it in sequence:

▶ whole;

▶ cut in half;

▶ peeled;

Then let them taste a piece.

Children could make observational drawings and complete a grid which asks a range of questions about their fruit or vegetable. For example:

What colours are on the outside of the fruit?	
What does the outside feel like?	
How is the inside different from the outside?	
How many different words can you use to describe how it tastes? Make a list.	

In this way you are offering a model to children for asking questions and question types. The activity could be repeated by offering children a piece of fruit if they had a vegetable and vice versa.

LITERACY LINK

When the activity is repeated children could create their own grid using a different set of questions. Discuss with children the types of questions that they could ask. As they have already had experience of this activity they will have something on which to model their responses. Challenge children to think of different questions to those they were offered originally. Ask them to think about the fruit or vegetable they have explored and to use what they found out to develop their questions. Also challenge children to ask questions with different stems, such as:

What?, Why?, How?, Does it?, Will it?

Provide children with a second grid already drawn so that they do not spend most of their time creating the grid rather than concentrating on the questions.

Place a range of unusual objects related to science on an activity table and have a box by the side into which children can 'post' questions. Open the 'question post box' at regular intervals during the week. Share the questions and give children the opportunity to answer them.

Asking questions ▸ ACTIVITY 8B: The solar system

SCIENCE LEARNING OUTCOME

▸ Extend personal knowledge about the solar system.

SCIENCE ACTIVITY

Have a brainstorming session to find out what the children already know about the solar system. Ask them to create a personal knowledge page on which they list everything they know on this topic and keep it to compare with a similar list at the end of the topic. This offers children an opportunity to reflect on how much work they have done and changes in their own understanding.

Encourage children to reflect on what they *already know* and to create a list of questions about things they *would like to know* on either the whole solar system, aspects of it, or a particular planet.

LITERACY LINK

At this level children should be familiar with questioning. The key issue should be children refining their own questions.

Give children a copy of the resource on page 90. Ask them to read the questions and think about the following:

▸ Which questions are open and which are closed?

▸ Can any of the closed questions be changed into open questions that would encourage research?

▸ How many different question stems have been used?

▸ Which questions can be changed to increase the range of question stems?

▸ Can they include additional questions with different stems?

Challenge children to use a similar approach to create their own list of questions.

When children have completed their questions they should be offered opportunities to answer them, using a range of reference material including books, CD-ROMs and the Internet. This provides an opportunity for children to develop their note-making skills.

TOPIC 9 ANSWERING QUESTIONS

KEY ISSUES

▶ Not only do children's questions need to be valued, but children also need to be confident that they will be given opportunities to answer them.

▶ Many children will need help to answer their questions, for example guidance on what to do or think about in order to answer a question.

▶ Children should appreciate that there is often more than one answer to a question.

▶ Children should be helped to appreciate that answers to questions are based on the science we know now, and that the answer might be different in future years as our scientific knowledge changes.

▶ Children should appreciate that we can answer different questions in different ways and that we do not always have to look in a book to find the answer.

▶ Children should be taught how to classify their questions in terms of how they might be answered, e.g. using a book, observing, using a CD-ROM, trying something out.

▶ Children need time to answer questions.

SUPPORTING STRATEGIES

▶ Offer children an 'answering questions board' where they sort the questions into groups according to whether they can be answered by using a book, by observing, or by trying something out.

▶ Share children's answers. For example, ask two children to answer the same question and share and compare their answers.

▶ Scaffold answering questions by asking children to log their questions, check them and suggest which book they might find useful for finding an answer.

▶ Provide a range of answers around the classroom that children have to search out.

▶ Organise 'answer the question hunts' where you or the children ask questions about science around the classroom and children have to find the answers from material in the classroom, such as books, wall displays, table-top activities or their own science exercise books or folders.

▶ Page 91 offers a photocopiable framework for answering questions.

Children's work

Provide children with the opportunity to answer their own questions through observation, investigations or research using a range of reference material.

Matthew O'B

16·03·98   Research   to   Answer   Questions

1. Venus' Diameter is 12,103 km (7,521) miles

2. We could not make our homes on venus because of the heat at 480°C

3. Galilao discovered Venus

4. because she was a roman goddess of love.

5. not much because most of it evapourates into acid clouds

6. We wouldn't ever be able to live on Venus

7. We would be roasted by heat, pushed over by Wind, suffocated by the thick air and poisoned by the acid clouds.

8. Venus is the second planet away from the sun. it is 108.1 million km away

9. it wouldn't be different at all

10. No, because they researched it and discovered that they would die before they got there

11. if the earth was 100% gravity, Venus would be 88% gravity

12. it is impossible to live on Venus.

Answering questions ▸ ## ACTIVITY 9A: Invertebrates

SCIENCE LEARNING OUTCOMES

▶ Know that invertebrates need certain things to live.

▶ Know that invertebrates have special features which do special jobs.

▶ Know that different invertebrates live in different habitats.

SCIENCE ACTIVITY

Children have observed an invertebrate and asked a range of questions, for example six, each written on a separate piece of paper or scribed by an adult assisting the individual. This activity offers support to enable children to decide how to answer their questions.

LITERACY LINK

Children are offered the following headings on a board or a table top:

Look	Think	Do	Book

The children read each of their questions in turn and think about how they might answer it. For example:

▶ **Look.** Look at their invertebrate to find the answer; for example, its colour, how it moves.

▶ **Think.** Do children already know the answer or can they work the answer out? For example, with the question *Are snails and slugs the same?* children who have seen both may be able to work the answer out for themselves.

▶ **Do.** Some questions will provide opportunities for children to test an idea. For example, *Which food does a snail like best?* might be answered by putting out two or three different foods and observing what happens. This offers the beginning of an investigation.

▶ **Book.** If the question cannot be answered by doing any of the above, looking in a book is probably the only way they will be able to answer their question.

When they have made their decision the children place their question under the appropriate heading. Children could then take all the questions under the **Look** heading and answer them, before moving on to the next category.

At some point give children the opportunity to share their questions and answers. If children are answering the same question they could compare their answers and also see who can add some more information to another person's answer.

Answering questions

ACTIVITY 9B: Venus

SCIENCE LEARNING OUTCOMES

▶ Know that there are different kinds of questions.

▶ Know that there are different ways to find the answers to questions.

SCIENCE ACTIVITY

Many aspects of science cannot be taught through 'hands-on practical work' and so children need to be introduced to other ways of answering their questions and solving problems. When children learn about Earth in Space much of the information can only be found out by using reference material. Being able to access and use reference material to answer questions in science is an important skill and one where children require support.

In this activity children are working in pairs to ask questions, find different ways of answering them and then design and make a double-page spread using their information for a class book on the solar system. Children should be given access to a range of resources which could include:

▶ posters;

▶ Internet;

▶ science non-fiction books;

▶ e-mail (e.g. talk to astronomers about their questions);

▶ videos;

▶ CD-ROMs.

One of the greatest challenges is to encourage children to represent information in their own words, rather than copy large sections of information or download chunks of text from CD-ROMs. Encouraging children to ask specific questions helps to minimise this, since it usually requires children to sift through reference material to find particular information. Giving children an audience (here a class book for other children to read) can focus their attention on how to represent

and communicate information to other children in an interesting way, for example: pictures, puzzles, jokes, information boxes, poems, wordsearches, strip cartoons, diagrams, fact-files, lift-up flaps with questions and answers, crosswords.

LITERACY LINK

Give children access to a range of resources related to the planet they are studying. In this example children could be given a specific piece of text containing information about their planet. Photocopiable page 92 contains information about Venus.

Ask children to read the material and highlight key points related to the different questions they have asked. They should make notes for each question and then think about the different ways they could present their answers. Children could write down a suggestion for how they could communicate the answer, on their double-page spread, beside each question. For example:

What is the position of Venus in the solar system?	Diagram
What does the planet look like?	Download photograph from CD-ROM
Who discovered Venus?	Lift up flap, question and answer

When children have answered each of their questions and made suggestions for how to represent their information, the next step is for them to design and make their double-page spread for the class book. At the draft stage, encourage children to review each other's work and engage in being 'critical friend', offering each other constructive comments.

TOPIC 10 POETRY

KEY ISSUES

▶ Science and the arts should not be separated. They have much to offer each other.

▶ Many children enjoy poems. They enjoy the sounds, the way words rhyme and features such as alliteration and repetition of words.

▶ Many poems have a scientific context (see pages 93 and 94) and can be used to illustrate ideas and phenomena in science.

▶ Children could be asked to describe something they have observed or science ideas in the form of a poem.

▶ Children will need experience of listening to many different kinds of poems but particularly science poems.

▶ Science poems can be:
- *read together;*
- *listened to on an audio-tape;*
- *part of a classroom display;*
- *the focus of a class book;*
- *read independently or with a friend.*

▶ Many poems can be linked to science themes such as weather, materials, sound or animals.

SUPPORTING STRATEGIES

▶ Encourage children to look for science poetry. Create a class science poetry book to which children can add poems.

▶ Children can be given a simple structure for writing a poem based on a set of questions. In this example the children were asked for words or phrases rather than whole sentences. Here a year 2 child was observing a woodlouse:

What is it?	*A woodlouse*
What colour is it?	*Grey*
What shape is it?	*Oval*
How does it move?	*Trundling along*
What does it remind you of?	*Like an army tank*

▶ Adopt a science poem and ask children to learn it off by heart.

▶ Purchase science poetry books for the class or school library and have a special 'science poetry week' where children read and are read a range of science-based poems.

▶ Use science-based poems as the starting point for a science lesson.

▶ Ask children to identify and explain the science in a poem.

Children's work

Children have used observations of plants to write their poems and they have also based poems on their own research – here, for example, research on the planets.

Jupiter

Jupiter and its swirling clouds of gas.
Unstoppable storms whirling on the surface of Jupiter.
Poisonous clouds cover the air.
Io with its volcanic eruptions and
The sulphur lakes.
Everywhere storms penetrate the surface of Jupiter
Rotating day and night Jupiter is still my favourite planet.

Y5/6, ST THOMAS MORE RC PRIMARY SCHOOL, DURHAM

Mercury

Much stony soil
Everlasting gases
Rocks reach across to the craters
Craters craters everywhere
Undisturbed planet
Rough with rocks and craters
Yet it is still there

Science can provide the context for some beautiful poems written by children. These examples illustrate how science has provided the stimulus for creative work of exceptional quality, indicating that the arts and science can and should share common ground.

Seeds that twist and seeds that twirl
Seeds with wings that spin and whirl
Seeds that float on thistledown
Seeds in coats of glossy brown
Seeds that burst with popping sound
From their pods to reach the ground
Seeds with hooks that clutch and cling
Seeds I plant for flowers next spring

Y5/6, GRANGE PARK PRIMARY SCHOOL, SUNDERLAND

Yellowy green anther holds the pollen
Tall filament keeping the anther high
Fragile stamens surrounding the lady
Sticky stigma collects the pollen
Hollow style swallows the pollen
Plump ovary protects the ovules
Sturdy carpel surrounding by the men
Attracted bluebells in the meadow.

Children can also share what they know through poems. In this example, a child describes and explains the parts of a plant's reproductive system.

Y2

ACTIVITY 10A: Melting chocolate

SCIENCE LEARNING OUTCOMES

▶ Know that heat causes some things to change.

▶ Know that heating some materials causes them to melt.

▶ Know that heating chocolate causes it to melt.

SCIENCE ACTIVITY

This activity is based on the Michael Rosen poem *Chocolate* on page 95. The poem provides a starting point for a range of activities, for example:

▶ a teacher demonstration of different substances being melted over a night-light, e.g. butter, chocolate, lard, margarine, wax, ice;

▶ simple investigations to find out which is the best place to keep chocolate;

▶ investigations to find the best way to stop ice lollies melting.

An introductory activity that explains how the poem *Chocolate* can be used is described below.

LITERACY LINK

There are several ways in which this poem could be used with children to develop the idea that heating some things can cause changes, and, in particular, that heating chocolate can make it melt. Perhaps the most interesting approach for children is to get one child or every child in the group to role-play the child in the poem. If only one child is used, take them aside and explain what they need to do, that is to hold a piece of chocolate (perhaps a chocolate button) so that it gradually melts. Do reassure the child that he or she will not get into trouble and ask if they mind licking the chocolate off their 'clean' fingers towards the end of the poem. If all of the children are involved the teacher simply needs to make sure that children's hands are clean and that they are washed at the end.

Invite the children holding a chocolate button to do exactly what the child in the poem does while you read it to them. Talk with them about what they think will happen and why, at suitable points. Discuss how the chocolate feels at the beginning of the poem and then later as the chocolate melts. Encourage children to describe the chocolate and what happens to it, using appropriate words, such as: *melt, change, warm, chocolate, sticky, messy, runny.*

Once the poem has been read and hands washed, re-read it and ask children to think about what the child in the poem could have done to the chocolate to stop it from melting. Scribe their ideas and then discuss how to test them in a simple investigation. Ask them to think about:

▶ What do we want to find out?

▶ What do you think you will have to do?

▶ Will you need any special equipment or materials?

▶ How will you make sure your tests are fair?

▶ How will you record your results?

Poetry ▶ ACTIVITY 10B: Parts of a flower

SCIENCE LEARNING OUTCOMES

▶ Know the parts of a flower.

▶ Be able to explain the function of parts of a flower.

SCIENCE ACTIVITY

Give children an outline of the flower (page 96) and ask them to use a range of reference material to find out the main parts of the flower and what each part does. The aim of this activity is for children to find out the role of each of the different parts of the flower in the reproduction of flowering plants.

Ask children to label the flower and create captions which give a brief description of the function of each of the different parts and their role in reproduction. Challenge children to make sure that they do not copy verbatim from books or CD-ROMs but reword explanations. Children could word-process their labels and captions and arrange them around the diagram of the flower.

LITERACY LINK–LITERACY HOUR

This Literacy Hour activity makes use of the information that children have researched in the above activity. Make sure that children have access to the reference material they have used, as well as their notes and their completed diagram of the parts of a flower. Give them a copy of the poem, *The Living Life of Plants*, on page 93. This activity is often more successful if children have a real flower, such as a buttercup, to look at, particularly since the children will be asked to describe the different parts of a flower.

SHARED TEXT WORK (15 MINS)

Ask children to read the poem on their own and then read it as a whole class. Discuss the poem with the children and ask them to think about:

▶ the structure of the poem;

▶ how each line combines a description of the part of the flower with what it does;

▶ whether the poem tells the whole story of reproduction and, if not, why?

Ask children to suggest lines for parts that they think the poem has not described and explained.

FOCUSED WORD AND SENTENCE WORK (15 MINS)

Make a list of the different parts of the flower and what they look like. Create a 'class poem' linking the parts of the flower, descriptions of what they look like and explanations of what they do. Ask children to consider each of the lines and how they can be made to flow and create a poem.

INDEPENDENT WRITING (20 MINS)

Challenge children to write their own poem about the life of a plant.

WHOLE-CLASS REVIEW (10 MINS)

Invite children to read out their own poems and comment on each other's poems using similar criteria to those used in the first part of this Literacy Hour.

TOPIC 11 ▶ MAKING NOTES

KEY ISSUES

▶ Note-making is not easy for children. They need to be taught how to do it effectively.

▶ Children need to be taught the purpose of note-making.

▶ Practice in note-making should be given at regular intervals and in a range of contexts. For example:
- *listening to a visitor and making notes about what he or she says;*
- *making notes about things observed in the environment;*
- *making notes about observations during an investigation to complement quantitative measurements.*

▶ Children who have difficulty in writing may be helped by provision of a tape-recorder (preferably hand-held) for them to speak into and produce a set of oral notes.

▶ Children will need to be taught when notes are appropriate. This means that the teacher will need to indicate when children should be making notes and provide regular opportunities for children to engage in note-making.

▶ The teacher will need to offer a range of strategies to support children in learning how to make notes.

▶ Children will need practice in identifying the important things to make notes about.

SUPPORTING STRATEGIES

▶ Ask children to carry out a short science activity and to make notes of the important things that happen. It is sometimes easier for children to learn how to make notes when they have to write about something they have experienced at first hand.

▶ Get children to read a short piece of information, pick out three main points and make a set of notes listing the three points.

▶ The resource on page 97 offers a photocopiable framework for making notes.

▶ Give children a newspaper article about a science-based event or discovery and ask them to create a set of notes of 4–6 key points from the article.

▶ Invite someone to be interviewed, perhaps on the subject of the children's current topic, such as an amateur astronomer. Children could take notes while the person is talking. Alternatively the interview could be video-taped for later viewing and note-making.

Children's work

Making notes

When you have read your information, make a list of the key ideas

1 The heart is one of the major organs

2 The " acts " as a pump.

3 it has two pumps one on left and on right

4 The left one pumps blood which contains oxygen it travels to right round body hand heart

5 Blood flows in same direction never backwards

6 Blood flows round the body this is called circulation

7 A heart beats approximately 70 times a minute

8 When your heart beats approx 7oml of blood goes through body

9 You get a wave of blood called a pulse

10 you need exercise to keep your heart fit

Here are two different approaches to note-making, using the text on the heart on page 98. As children develop the ability to make notes they should be encouraged to abbreviate words and note the source of the information.

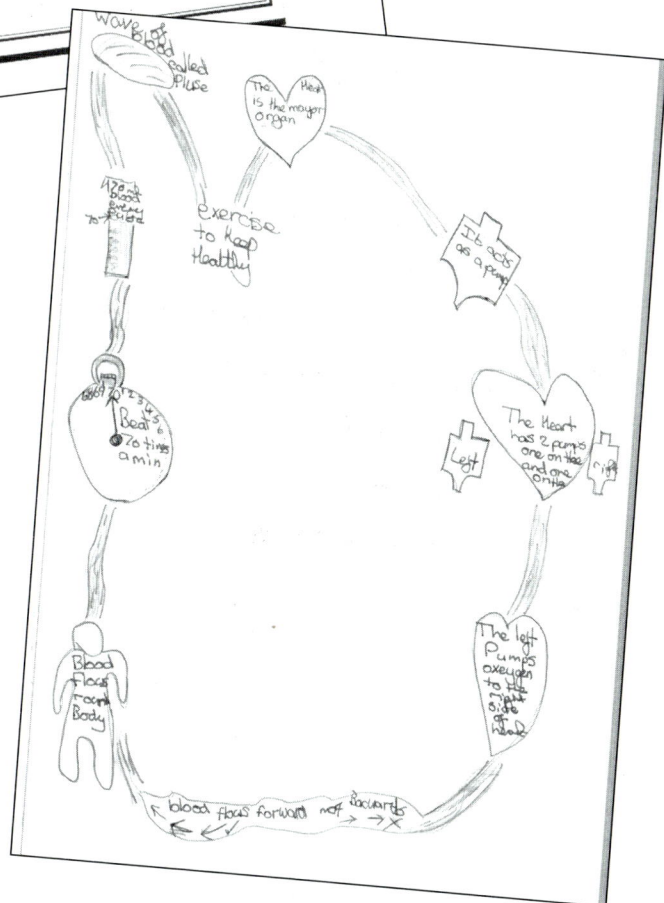

Y5, ST THOMAS MORE RC PRIMARY SCHOOL, DURHAM

Y2

ACTIVITY 11A: Manufactured materials

SCIENCE LEARNING OUTCOMES

▶ Know that some materials are manufactured.

▶ Know how some materials are made.

▶ Know that the same material can be used for different objects.

SCIENCE ACTIVITY

Children develop their own ideas about materials and their origins. This activity is based on work from the Nuffield Primary Science book *Materials* (Collins), which suggests an approach for eliciting children's understanding about how materials and objects are made.

Give children a sheet of paper divided into 6–8 sections. Ask them to tell, in a set of pictures, the story of an object, such as a spoon or a glass, from the origin of the material or materials of which it is made to the finished product.

Discuss with children their ideas on how a particular object was made, looking for similarities and differences. Ask them to justify what they have put, where possible drawing on evidence they might be able to offer, such as personal experience.

Provide children with access to either non-fiction books of an appropriate level or video or CD-ROM material. Ask them to use the reference material to find out the key stages in making the material under discussion.

LITERACY LINK

Children need to be taught how to make notes. Offer them a table which focuses on the main points and demands that they only use a few key words, for instance:

Glass is made from...	sand and silica
To make glass the first thing they do is...	
Then they...	
After that they...	
Finally they...	
We have these things made from glass:	

Ask children to use the information they have recorded in their tables to draw a new version of their original piece of work about how a material is made. Encourage them to compare their first attempt with their new set of pictures and to talk about the similarities and differences, comparing what they know now with what they knew before they carried out their research.

Making notes

ACTIVITY 11B: The heart

SCIENCE LEARNING OUTCOMES

▶ Know the key organs of the body.

▶ Know the functions of different organs of the body.

SCIENCE ACTIVITY

As part of work on the body children should be encouraged to access a range of information about the major organs and their positions in the body as well as their functions. Children should be given access to reference material such as videos, books, posters, health leaflets and CD-ROMs. To ensure that they make notes effectively and encourage them to engage with text sources, it is useful to teach children the rudiments of note-making by offering opportunities to practise this skill during Literacy Hours. Children can then use similar approaches during their science lesson to research information about other organs of the body.

LITERACY LINK–LITERACY HOUR

The photocopiable material on 'The Heart' on pages 98 and 99 can be used for this activity.

SHARED TEXT WORK (15 MINS)
Give children photocopies of the page of information on the heart. Ask them to read the material and, using a pencil or a highlighter, mark key words and phrases on their page. Discuss what they have chosen as the key words and phrases and mark these on an OHP.

FOCUSED WORD AND SENTENCE WORK (15 MINS)
Ask children to use the text they have highlighted to create a set of key points about the heart, placing them in order and rewording where necessary.

INDEPENDENT WRITING (20 MINS)
Give the children a copy of the diagram of the heart. Ask them to use their notes (and the original text) to annotate the outline of the heart with appropriate labels and to write captions giving key information relating to how the heart works. The result should be an annotated diagram based on the information from the text. Children should be asked to make sure that annotations:

▶ are appropriate;

▶ are concise;

▶ make sense.

WHOLE-CLASS REVIEW (10 MINS)
Several children in turn could place their labelled and annotated heart drawing on an OHP as a basis for discussion during the whole-class review session. Ask children to play 'critical friend', saying what they considered to be the most important information to include on the diagram and offering constructive comments on how others structured their annotations. Where appropriate, encourage children to re-word annotations to develop quality in written work.

TOPIC 12 ▶ INSTRUCTIONAL TEXT

KEY ISSUES

▶ Instructional text is a set of instructions explaining how to do something.

▶ Writing instructions challenges children to:
- *sequence events;*
- *make decisions about what information should be included and what should be discarded;*
- *be concise;*
- *consider the audience.*

▶ Children need to experience different types of instructions, e.g. recipes, strip-cartoon instructions, prose.

▶ Children should be given a real reason for creating a set of instructions; for example, a recipe for another group to use, instructions on how to set up an electric circuit or how to make a switch for an electric circuit.

▶ Children should write instructions for someone else to use; for example, someone in the class or younger children.

▶ Children should be given feedback on how useful their instructions were to someone else: how easy they were to use, whether they lead to success and how they could be improved.

SUPPORTING STRATEGIES

▶ Discuss the layout of instructions with children. Ask them to consider:
- *How clear are the instructions?*
- *How are the instructions set out?*
- *How are the instructions worded?*
- *Are there any illustrations? If so, what do they show?*

Page 100 provides a resource for this activity.

▶ Ask children to create instructions about something tangible, such as a set of instructions for making a circuit.

▶ Give children a specific audience for which to create instructions, such as another class. Let the class try out the instructions and provide feedback.

▶ Create a class or whole-group set of instructions and then ask children to follow their own instructions and edit and change the instructions to improve them.

▶ Analyse with children different ways of producing and presenting instructions, including special features such as:
- *use of numbers to show the order in which things are done;*
- *use of words such as: After you have, Next, When you have, Make sure that;*
- *use of diagrams or pictures.*

▶ Create a 'giant display' set of instructions as a class. Label them to indicate formatting and special features included to help the user.

▶ As a method of recording and communicating their science investigation, challenge one group to communicate their investigation to another group by means of instructions, so that the other group can use the instructions to carry out the same investigation. Allow children time to give feedback on the instructions created by the other group.

Instructional text

Children's work

In this example children have created a fire safety leaflet which includes instructions on what to do when discovering a fire so that occupants can leave a house safely . They had to consider who their audience was and how to make the information look interesting so that it would be read.

FIRE SAFETY

By 5L, Ashley Primary School

Fighting fire!

ASHLEY ROAD PRIMARY SCHOOL, TYNESIDE. (EXAMPLE TAKEN FROM FEASEY, R. AND SIRAJ-BLATCHFORD, J. (1998) *KEY SKILLS: COMMUNICATION IN SCIENCE.* UNIVERSITY OF DURHAM AND TYNESIDE TEC.)

Combustion-Fire!

A leading fire fighter, Trevor Smith, came into our class to talk about fire safety
A fire needs three things to start.
These three things are oxygen, fuel and heat.
Without one of them the fire will go out.
We did some tests to prove this.
1) Mr Smith lit a candle and put a jar over it.
The flame went out.
This was because there was no oxygen in the jar.
2) Mr Smith lit a match and let it burn. When it reached the end, the flame went out. This was because the fuel had ran out.
3) Mr Smith lit a candle and blew it out. The breath was cold and cooled the heat.
By Kate Hutchinson and Nicholas Dodds

INSIDE...

*Our experiment, - page 2,
The Fire Rules,
Escape Routes - page 3,
Wordsearch and poems - page 4*

OUR FIRE RULES

1) If a fire occurs in your house:
GET OUT, CALL THE FIRE BRIGADE OUT AND STAY OUT!
2) Keep calm
3) If there is a pet or another person in the house don't go back inside.
4) If the fire catches your clothes don't run, it will only make it worse, get down on the ground and roll.

5) Make sure you have a smoke detector and test it every month.
6) If there is smoke stay low to the ground.
7) Make sure you have an escape route, and make sure there are no toys in the way.
8) Don't smoke and don't play with matches.
By Nicholas Dodds and Kate Hutchinson

HOTLINE 999

GET A PLAN!

We thought if a fire broke out in our house how would we get out. If the fire was on the stairs I would go through my bedroom on to the landing and go into the bathroom and jump out the window on to the balcony.
By Simon Le Touze and Jessica Hall

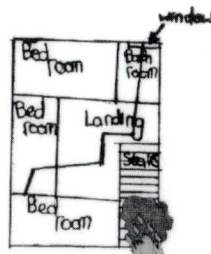

KEEP SAFE - CHECK YOUR CURTAINS!

FABRICS BURNING BY NICHOLAS DODDS
Some of our clothes and furnishing materials are made from fabrics which are flame resistant.
This means that they are not easily set on fire.
Some fabrics, however, flare up when a flame touches them. Other fabrics melt.
So we set about testing different materials.
We did two experiments to find out the safest material to make curtains and pyjamas.
CURTAINS: First we got five fabrics and made sure they were all the same size for fair testing.
The fabrics were nylon, satin, padding, glazed cotton and mixed cotton .
Then we tested them by taking turns at holding the tongs, lighting them then copying our observations onto a sheet .
PYJAMAS : We repeated this test with different fabrics, which were: elasticated cotton, stretch nylon and rayon, knitted cotton, nylon and cotton.
Here are two tables of our results.

CURTAIN MATERIAL	NYLON	SATIN	PADDING	GLAZED COTTON	MIXED COTTON
Does the fabric light easily?	YES	NO	YES	NO	NO
Does it burn quickly or slowly?	Very quickly	Quite quickly	Very quickly	Does not burn	Quite quickly
What is left at the end?	Hard, crispy smooth ash	Feels like hard tar or plastic	Bubbling ash and hard cinder	Black material	Very crispy, quite smooth ash

PYJAMA MATERIAL	ELASTICATED COTTON	STRETCHED NYLON	KNITTED COTTON	NYLON/ RAYON	COTTON
Does the fabric light easily?	YES	YES	YES	NO	YES
Does it burn quickly or slowly?	Very quickly	Melted quickly	Slowly	Slowly	Very quickly
What is left at the end?	Crunchy ash	Hard tar	Very crumbly, powdery material	Yellow tar	Smouldering white ash

Instructional text

ACTIVITY 12A: Electricity

SCIENCE LEARNING OUTCOMES

▶ Know that a complete circuit is needed to make a lamp (bulb) light.

▶ Be able to draw a circuit picture.

SCIENCE ACTIVITY

This activity is for use towards the end of work on electricity and circuits and can provide an assessment point. The children make a complete circuit so that a component, such as a lamp or a motor, works. They then create a set of instructions for someone else to use to make the same circuit.

LITERACY LINK

Children will need some support in creating instructions. They may have seen different kinds of instructions in recent Literacy Hours. If they have, remind them what instructions are for and the different formats they can take. For example:

▶ strip cartoon;

▶ set of written points;

▶ series of diagrams.

Discuss with children what they think are the important things to include in their set of instructions and what they should be like. For example:

▶ be clear;

▶ have pictures with labels;

▶ describe step by step;

▶ have sentences to explain;

▶ include a list of equipment.

When children have finished they should give their set of instructions to a friend to use to make the circuit. Their friend should comment on whether the instructions were easy to follow and suggest any improvements.

A nice finishing touch, which can also be used as an assessment record, is to offer a small certificate of achievement for creating a set of instructions for a circuit that works.

Instructional text

ACTIVITY 12B: Day and night

SCIENCE LEARNING OUTCOME

▶ Understand about day and night.

SCIENCE ACTIVITY

In this activity children research 'day and night' using a variety of reference material, including videos, books, CD-ROMs and posters. The children then model how they think day and night occur, using the knowledge and understanding gained from their research including how other people model day and night. The aim is to create a set of instructions for someone else to follow to enable them to teach others about day and night.

Children could use a digital camera to take a series of photographs of, for example, children modelling day and night using a globe. These photographs could then form part of the instructions.

Ask children what kind of vocabulary they should include in their instructions and whether they think any of the scientific words will need explaining. for example:

rotate	darkness
axis	twilight
Earth	dawn
Sun	length
tilt	globe
day	torch
night	model person
hours	

LITERACY LINK

The children will need to think about the purpose of instructional text. Do discuss this with children and, where appropriate, remind them of any work they have done on instructions in Literacy Hours. Ask children to identify the important features of a good set of instructions. They might suggest some of the following:

▶ correct information;

▶ clear pictures or diagrams;

▶ carefully chosen words;

▶ use of technical vocabulary;

▶ good explanations;

▶ reasons given as well as instructions;

▶ clear presentation;

▶ careful sequencing.

When children have drafted their set of instructions on how day and night occur, ask them to give it to someone else in the class who is prepared to take on a 'critical friend' role and try out the instructions. Encourage children to offer constructive criticism that can be incorporated into the final piece of work.

TOPIC 13 ▶ DEVELOPING PERSUASIVE ARGUMENT

KEY ISSUES

▶ Children need to develop the ability to appreciate that some people have different points of view in science.

▶ It is important that children are able to develop an argument based on reasoning and evidence in science.

▶ Children need opportunities to put forward their own point of view in a 'safe' environment.

▶ Children need to develop the ability to argue a point in a positive and constructive way.

▶ Children will have to:

- *offer arguments and reasons for their point of view;*
- *listen to the views and evidence offered by other people;*
- *consider their own views and ideas in the light of those of others;*
- *be prepared sometimes to change their own view, and see this as positive.*

SUPPORTING STRATEGIES

▶ Give children opportunities to offer their opinions on a topical subject.

▶ Offer newspaper headlines and articles for discussion.

▶ Engage children in debates where they have to take one side and argue a point.

▶ Within each science topic offer a controversial element so that children are regularly exposed to discussion and argument. For example:

- *electricity – building a wind farm next to the school;*
- *ourselves – cloning.*

▶ Allow children to analyse newspaper stories, television interviews, and so on, to find out how arguments are formed and phrased.

▶ Get children to create 'for' and 'against' tables listing the arguments for each side of the issue.

▶ Offer openers and connectives to support children in debating and developing a persuasive argument. For example:

- *The evidence suggests that...*
- *In my opinion...*
- *The facts speak for themselves.*

Photocopiable page 101 provides some examples.

Children's work

Louise

Is	it	fair?		yeas		be
case		they		have		booth
got		tranis		ond		they
are	the		same	haye		

Developing persuasive argument in science begins very early, in fact as soon as children begin school. It is important that children use their knowledge and experiences to justify what they think and say. For example, if children think that an investigation is fair they should be asked to justify what they say and offer evidence.

Y2, MURTON PRIMARY SCHOOL, SEAHAM, CO.DURHAM

Lets conserve it so they can observe it

Your Local area

In your local area there are alot of things you could do. Even in your own garden there are many possibilities like a bird nest box where many birds can nest in. It is also a good place for you to watch them. You could also donate a small part of your garden for a nature reserve, that could provide shelter, food, and a great place for you to enjoy nature just a few metres away. In Oxford they cleared some allotments to make a nature reserve. Now they are more important than ever. Planting a tree is a simple but a very effective way to provide food.

An excellent piece of homework

Environmental issues offer good contexts for children to use and develop persuasive argument. Here the argument is very subtle but nonetheless effective!

Y4/5, ISIS CE PRIMARY SCHOOL, OXFORD

ACTIVITY 13A: Best car

SCIENCE LEARNING OUTCOMES

▶ Be able to carry out a whole investigation.

▶ Be able to use evidence to support conclusions.

SCIENCE ACTIVITY

Ask children to bring in one or more toy cars and begin by discussing which car they think would travel the furthest if placed on a ramp and why. Choose four or five cars and ask the children to put them in order of which they think would come first, second, third, etc. Make a note of their predictions.

Challenge children to suggest how they could test their predictions. They may need access to a limited range of equipment to aid their planning. A planning framework, such as the planning house or train on page 31, may also be useful.

The children now carry out their investigation and record the results in a table. Depending on the abilities and needs of the children the investigation can offer many opportunities for developing different aspects of investigative work; for example, fair testing, measuring or recording data. Here the focus is on the feedback session where children consider their results and draw conclusions. An important aspect of investigative work is that children should be able to interrogate their data, talk or write about it and use their results to explain their conclusions.

When children have completed the practical part of the activity provide time for them to create a simple bar graph using the data in their table. This helps children to see differences more clearly and can make information more visible to other children, if large graph paper is used.

LITERACY LINK

Although 'persuasive argument' is an aspect of literacy that has prominence in the upper primary years it is important that children begin to use both scientific knowledge and data to persuade others (and themselves) that their conclusions are appropriate.

In this activity children generate data from their investigation and should use this evidence to support their conclusions. A selected range of openers and connectives can help children to articulate an argument. For example:

▶ My results show that...

▶ If we look at the table we can see that...

▶ The graph shows that...

▶ I noticed that...

▶ We can see from the table that the best is....

Offer openers and connectives as part of a large wall display or a table-top sheet or card. During the feedback session, when children talk about their investigation and results, ask children to use specific openers, for example:

Who can use 'My results show that....' in a sentence?

Developing persuasive argument ▶ ACTIVITY 13B: Environmental issues

SCIENCE LEARNING OUTCOMES

▶ Understand that an environment is a system that can be changed and damaged.
▶ Understand that food chains show how animals depend on each other and on plants.

SCIENCE ACTIVITY

The photocopiable material on page 102 offers the fictional scenario where a local community is debating whether or not houses and an industrial estate should be built on a Site of Special Scientific Interest. Children have to apply knowledge and understanding of food chains and habitats to develop arguments on the issues raised by the planning application to reclaim the pond and marsh area.

Ask the children to read the material and consider the arguments for and against the filling in of the gravel pits and drainage of the marsh area to provide land for development. Encourage them to consider all sides of the argument: the human cost in terms of lost opportunities for regenerating an ailing village by providing additional housing and employment, as well as the cost to the environment.

At the end of the activity each group presents its case to the rest of the class in whatever way it feels is appropriate. Encourage the groups to use a variety of different ways to present their case, for example:

▶ give a talk;

▶ produce a brochure;

▶ role-play a mock television or radio interview.

Challenge children who are arguing against the development to offer scientific evidence in the form of food chains to explain what would happen to plants and animals if the pond and marsh areas were destroyed.

To encourage children to engage with the issues and the debate offer each child a 'paper' vote to cast on behalf of either side.

LITERACY LINK

Some children might need support in developing arguments for and against the proposed development. Where appropriate children could use the photocopiable 'debating frame' on page 103 in conjunction with the information page. Encourage children to include their own ideas as well as those offered in the information text.

TOPIC 14 ▶ READING AND MAKING SCIENCE NON-FICTION BOOKS

KEY ISSUES

▶ Children should read a wide range of science non-fiction books.

▶ Children should have access to a wide range of science non-fiction books as a part of their everyday classroom environment.

▶ The teacher should be a positive role model for the children, reading and introducing them to a range of science non-fiction.

▶ The teacher should aim to make science non-fiction as popular with children as fiction books.

▶ Children should develop an understanding of the function and structure of science non-fiction books.

▶ Children should be offered opportunities to be literary critics, not only of fiction books but also of science non-fiction. They should create critiques of science non-fiction books on a regular basis throughout the primary years.

▶ If possible children should be introduced to 'real' authors of science non-fiction books so that they can discuss how non-fiction authors research a topic and write their books.

▶ The profile and status of science non-fiction books should be raised in the classroom and they should become a regular feature of children's learning in science.

SUPPORTING STRATEGIES

▶ Use science non-fiction books as class readers instead of fiction books.

▶ Give children opportunities to consider how information is presented in non-fiction books. Ask them to look through a book and list the different methods used; for example, diagrams, photographs, prose, lists, glossaries. They can then use their list to choose different approaches to representing their own information from research.

▶ Discuss with children the different ways in which information is presented, including CD-ROM. Talk about why different kinds of information need to be presented in different ways. For example, numerical information is often better presented in a table or as a graph; photographs or diagrams can provide a lot of information; other information is often better presented as prose.

▶ Create a science non-fiction book. A whole book is often too much for individual children or small groups, but children can be asked to create a single page or a double-page spread for a class book.

▶ Allow children to choose and adopt a science non-fiction book, read it and get to know it in detail. Ask them to create a two-minute presentation to convince another person to buy it. Hold a class 'Book Auction' with the 'sellers' giving their presentations, and children using pretend book tokens to 'buy' the book they choose. (See page 108 for book token.)

▶ Photocopiable resource pages 104 to 107 offer suggestions for making books in science.

Children's work

Children can make small books in science or create pages for a class book. Their books can include their own ideas and reports of their investigations as well as material that they have researched using a range of non-fiction material.

Planet

Fact File

by Ashley Rich

Contents

Planet	Page
Mercury	2-3
Venus	3-4
Earth	4-5
Mars	5-6
Jupiter	6-7
Saturn	7-8
Uranus	8-9
Neptune	9-10
Pluto	10-11

Jupiter

Facts

1 Jupiter is the largest planet in the solar system. A day in Jupiter is 9 hours and 50 minutes long

Y4, ISIS CE PRIMARY SCHOOL, OXFORD

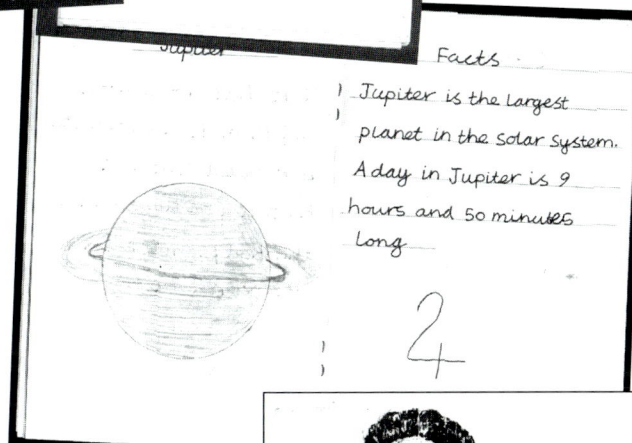

To help children understand the nature and purpose of science non-fiction they should be given opportunities to analyse and be critical of reference books and other material such as information on CD-ROMs.

Emily   Science Books   16th March 1998.

The Science Encyclopaedia has lots of facts in it, and would probably be used for reference for exams. This book is probably for older children, as some of the language is quite hard to grasp. However, the 'Fatal Forces' book is totally different. The Isaac Newton story is really written like one. You would use this book just for light reading to learn, as the text is very easy to take in.
The Encyclopaedia has the title 'Newton, Isaac.' I think that this is because it is easier to look up the second name than the first, as lots of people have the same first name. You do not need to do this in the 'Fatal Forces' book because you just read through it, it is all on one subject and you do not have to look things up. The Encyclopaedia states more dates than the 'Fatal Forces' book.
The similarities are; well, obviously, they are both about the same thing! They do mention similar things but the Fatal Forces book goes into a lot more detail.
I think that the Encyclopaedia is written for older children because it throws facts at you. The Fatal Forces book is funnier, and it is as if the author is talking to you.
I think that the fatal forces does it's job very well, as it really appealed to me. The encyclopaedia was very good as a source of information, and would be very interesting if you were studying for an exam. I think that I preferred Fatal Forces,

Y6, LLANTILIO PERTHOLEY PRIMARY SCHOOL, ABERGAVENNY

ACTIVITY 14A: Invertebrates

SCIENCE LEARNING OUTCOMES

▶ Understand how invertebrates can be identified and classified.

▶ Know that animals need certain things to stay alive.

▶ Know how to carry out a detailed observation of an animal.

SCIENCE ACTIVITY

A series of activities can lead up to children creating a book on invertebrates. The activities begin with children going out into the school grounds looking for invertebrates. They record where different invertebrates can be found and how many are seen in each place, either on a map or a simple two-column table. Then children carefully collect one invertebrate and produce an observational drawing, returning the invertebrate to its habitat when the drawing is complete.

In the classroom, individual children 'adopt' an invertebrate, perhaps the one they have drawn, and make a list of questions to which they would like to know the answers, and research information using a range of reference material.

All of the material children have produced can be used as part of either a class or individual book on invertebrates.

LITERACY LINK

Carefully analyse some science non-fiction books with the children to find out what most of them have in common; for example, contents, information, pictures, photographs, glossary, index. This can provide a model for the class big book.

Give children a personal 'mini-book' so that they can mirror how the class book was made and make their own. The mini-book should not contain more than 8 pages but should be able to be extended where appropriate. To support children, write a question at the top of each page for them to answer. The question could be the same for every child or the children could ask their own questions and write them in or have an adult scribe for them.

Children then use books to find the answers to each of their questions. Encourage them to use illustrations in books as well as text to find the answers.

When children have completed their book ask them to compare it with one of the non-fiction books they have been using. Then ask them to think about what to put on the front and back covers of their own mini-book. Allow children to read and share each other's books and comment on what they like about each book, what they find interesting, and so on.

Reading and making science non-fiction books

ACTIVITY 14B: The solar system

SCIENCE LEARNING OUTCOMES

▶ Know more about the solar system.

▶ Know more about individual planets in the solar system.

SCIENCE ACTIVITY

Encourage children to brainstorm what they know about the solar system, either through creating a list or concept mapping. As a whole class, in pairs or individually allow children to think about what they do not know and what they would like to know. Ask them to create a list of questions; for example, the ten things they would like to know about the Sun, Pluto or red dwarfs.

Offer children a variety of resources to research the answers to their questions. They should have access to CD-ROMs, Internet, textbooks, posters and video material. If possible, contact a local astronomical society or university department to establish links that would allow children to write letters to or e-mail an 'expert' with their questions.

LITERACY LINK

Give children the opportunity to use the information they have gathered to write a mini-topic of their own in the form of a book or to create a class book where individuals or pairs are responsible for a double-page spread.

Challenge children to:

▶ decide on the content and how it is to be organised;

▶ use information they have researched to answer their questions;

▶ consider how they will present their information in an interesting way;

▶ create a draft page layout and receive 'critical friend' comment from other people;

▶ produce their page using a desk-top publishing package;

▶ create contents, glossary, information about the book and authors, publishing information and ISBN number.

An important aspect of either a class or an individual book is the idea of an audience. It helps if children are given an audience for which to write. For example, it might be a group of younger children, a parents' evening or local library. Offering children an audience for their work helps to define what should be included in a book, the level at which it should be written and what kind of presentation would be appropriate.

TOPIC 15 ▶ WRITING IN NEWSPAPER STYLE

KEY ISSUES

▶ Children need experience of reading newspaper articles about science.

▶ Children should appreciate that a newspaper article tells a factual story.

▶ Newspaper articles offer an important source of information about current issues, inventions and innovations in science.

▶ Children should appreciate that newspaper articles may be exaggerated, tell only one side of a story or contain factual errors.

▶ Newspaper articles are often used to offer different points of view about an issue.

▶ Newspaper articles often have a particular construction which includes main headlines, paragraph sub-headings, introduction, main information and conclusion.

▶ Unlike newspaper reports of events based on direct observation, science articles are often based on one or two key ideas from a journal article or comments from 'experts' in the field of interest.

▶ Children should therefore consider the sources of information for newspaper articles and be encouraged to research, using books, CD-ROMs, videos and leaflets, as well as interviewing people.

SUPPORTING STRATEGIES

▶ Collect newspaper articles and headings with a science content.

▶ Create a newspaper article scrapbook or notice board on which the teacher and children can add current articles.

▶ Use newspaper articles regularly for class reading sessions and for discussion of the style, content and issues raised.

▶ Use newspaper articles as a starting point for classroom debates, where children have to present their own point of view or evaluate the argument and ideas offered in the article.

▶ Look at a range of newspaper headlines related to science and ask children to create newspaper headlines for their own investigation or area of research.

▶ Ask children to create a headline for a particular story. They might create several and decide which one they think is best and explain why.

▶ Working individually or in pairs ask children to write a newspaper article on a specific science story, event or issue or on their own findings from an investigation.

▶ Challenge children to use a computer newspaper package.

Children's work

The science topic 'pets' provided the stimulus for this piece of unaided writing using a newspaper format.

'Lost dog!

I lost my dog.

It was in the garden.

It is brown.

Please bring it to Downsell School

R, DOWNSELL PRIMARY SCHOOL, LONDON

Older children have a deeper understanding of written styles associated with newspapers. Children could write about past and present science inventions, people and environmental issues.

This article includes headline, photograph, introductory paragraph, information and an imaginary interview.

Y6, ST THOMAS MORE RC PRIMARY SCHOOL, DURHAM

The Daily Paper

20 Vol. 12 No. 24 August 25, 19 7

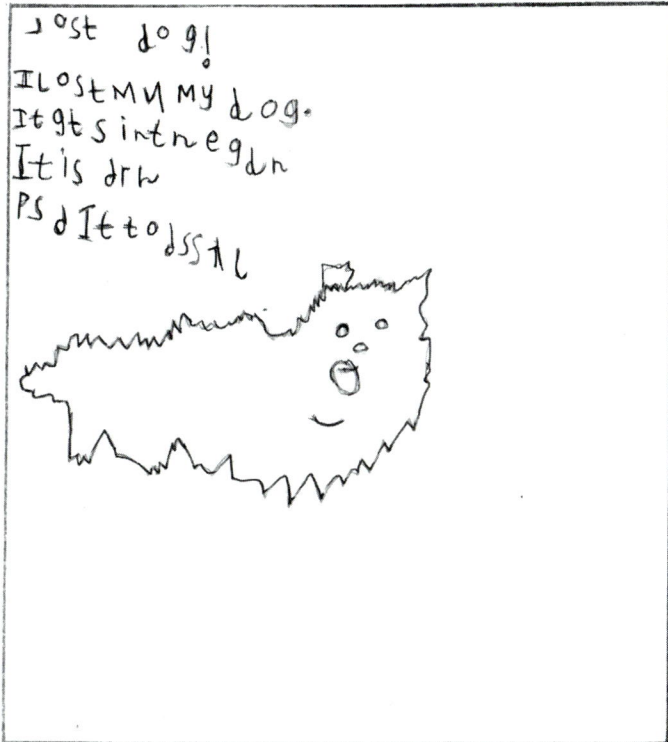

Jost dog!
ILostMyMy dog.
It gts in the egdn
It is drw
Psd It to dssl

E.C. TIMES
— 22.02.1878 —

LIGHTS CAMERA ACTION

Yesterday the inventor Thomas Edison created a new phenomenon, the parallel circuit.

People all over the world are all desparate to own this circuit. Edison was overwhelmed by supporters, the press and parties of paparazzi yesterday evening.
Edison's inspiration came from his laboratory when working last weekend. Thomas's vison for the futue will be that people will be able to use this circuit not only for lights around the house but for cookers and clocks and

for many other inventions still unknown.
Written and edited by
Miss Emily Coppen

LIGHT BULBS ON SALE NOW

Writing in newspaper style Activity 15A: Materials and uses

SCIENCE LEARNING OUTCOMES

▶ Know that materials have certain properties.

▶ Know that different materials do different jobs.

SCIENCE ACTIVITY

Read to children the story of *The Three Little Pigs*. Talk about the different materials used. Focus on the properties of the materials mentioned, what kind of things they can be used for and why bricks are best for building a house.

Provide children with opportunities to investigate the properties of different materials. For example:

▶ Is it waterproof?

▶ How strong is it?

Children could, for example, test a range of materials to find out which is the best for a roof, or which pattern of bricks is the strongest for building a wall.

LITERACY LINK

Offer children a range of newspaper headlines and ask them to discuss the headlines and what they tell the reader. The headlines could be real ones from newspapers, or headlines that the teacher has invented. Ask the children to think about each headline:

▶ Is it interesting?

▶ Does it tell the reader something about the story?

▶ Why is the headline short and not a long sentence?

Then ask the children to think about *The Three Little Pigs* story. Only one Little Pig made a house strong enough to protect him from the wolf. Ask children to make up their own headlines about the materials and the houses that the Little Pigs built. For example:

▶ Foolish Pig Builds House of Straw

▶ House of Sticks Collapses

Ask children to consider:

▶ What do they want to tell people in their headline?

▶ Is the headline interesting?

▶ Will the headline make people want to read more about the Little Pigs?

▶ What kind of words could be used to describe the Little Pigs?

▶ What kind of words could be used to describe the different properties of the materials, e.g. strong bricks, sturdy bricks?

The children might find it easier to offer their own ideas if the teacher provides some examples and then the children work as a whole class or group on several headlines.

Finally, the newspaper headlines could be used as part of a display related to science work based on materials and *The Three Little Pigs* story.

Writing in newspaper style > ## Activity 15B: Science inventors

SCIENCE LEARNING OUTCOMES

▶ Knowledge about scientists linked to the topic being studied.

▶ An appreciation of how scientists develop ideas, invent and discover things.

SCIENCE ACTIVITY

Children should be exposed to the culture and history of science during their primary years. Some topics offer a wide variety of interesting people. The stories of discoveries and inventions provide another dimension to children's scientific experience, helping them to appreciate that science is about people having ideas, taking risks and persevering.

Topics such as forces, electricity and light provide a wealth of opportunities for children to research the scientists behind developments in these areas. Give children access to a range of non-fiction material, including books, videos and CD-ROMs.

LITERACY LINK—LITERACY HOUR

This could provide activities to fill several Literacy Hours to give sufficient time for children to create a whole newspaper article. The management of the set of activities in the Literacy Hour depends on the experience and ability of children. Some children will be capable of using a variety of resources to research information on a particular scientist. Others might benefit from being restricted to one source of information. Children's notes from their research provide the basic information from which they will construct their newspaper article on their chosen scientist.

SHARED TEXT WORK (15 MINS)

Give children the photocopiable newspaper article on page 109 on which to base a discussion of the structure of a newspaper article. Encourage them to consider:

▶ layout;

▶ headline;

▶ sub-headings;

▶ use of paragraphs;

▶ flow of information, e.g. introduction, middle, conclusion.

Discuss with children what the public need to know about the scientist and his or her work, and what kind of things they would find interesting.

FOCUSED WORD AND SENTENCE WORK (15 MINS)

Ask children to create their headlines and sub-headings, using the latter as organisers for the information they have collected on their scientist.

INDEPENDENT WRITING (20 MINS)

Challenge children to write the paragraphs to go under each of their sub-headings. They should draft and redraft work, check spelling, grammar, and so on.

WHOLE-CLASS REVIEW (10 MINS)

Share different aspects of the newspaper articles, such as headlines, sub-headings, well-constructed paragraphs. Encourage children to take the role of 'critical friend', particularly in analysing why someone's headline is interesting, sub-headings flow or a paragraph is well written.

When children have completed their draft article they should be allowed to use appropriate ICT packages to create a front page of a newspaper. This process will demand that they edit their work and have access to desk-top publishing facilities.

TOPIC 16 ▶ LETTERS

KEY ISSUES

▶ Children should appreciate that different types of people write letters and that letter writing has a place in science.

▶ Letters provide an opportunity to write in a different genre in science for a range of audiences.

▶ Letters demand communication with a person or persons in a different location.

▶ Letters require clear expression of a limited number of ideas.

▶ Letters can be used for different purposes; for example, to give information, offer information in reply to a letter, offer a point of view.

▶ Letters have a particular format. Business letters give additional information such as a subject heading, telephone, fax and e-mail numbers.

▶ The composition of a letter is important and children should be offered opportunities to draft and redraft their letters.

▶ Where possible children should have a 'real' audience to write for.

▶ Before children write letters they should consider the purpose of the letters:
  - *Why are they writing?*
  - *What do they hope their letter will achieve?*

▶ Ask children to think about the audience:
  - *What will the person receiving the letter need to know?*
  - *What do you want the person to do?*

▶ A reply to a request or expression of a point of view will be eagerly awaited by children and provide a focus for interest that can be very motivating.

SUPPORTING STRATEGIES

▶ Contact a local company or someone in the community who would be willing to write to the children and receive and answer a letter or letters from the children. This gives an air of authenticity to their work and ensures that they are writing letters for a purpose and to an audience.

▶ Help children to word-process letters so their work looks more 'official'.

▶ Provide opportunities for children to write a range of letters in science; for example, asking questions, seeking specific data or information, giving information.

▶ Teach children how to include enclosures such as graphs or diagrams.

▶ Collect examples of letters from different people, such as industry, local councils, colleges and universities, to offer models for letter writing.

▶ Allow children to create their own letter-heads; for example:
Class 6 Scientific Research Establishment.

▶ Give children a letter that asks a question or poses a problem as a starting point for their science activity, such as photocopiable page 110. Ask them to reply by letter explaining what they did and found out.

As part of a project to develop a mini-woodland in their school grounds, children visited a woodland and met countryside ranger Stuart Bonar. They followed up their visit by writing letters to request further information.

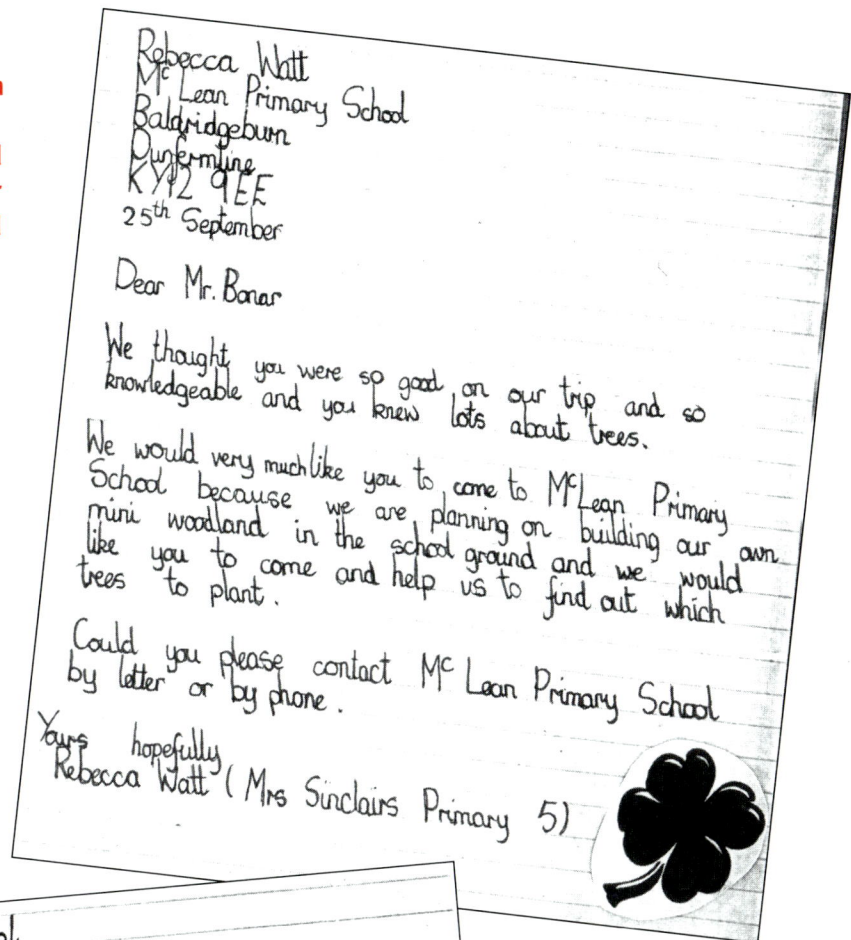

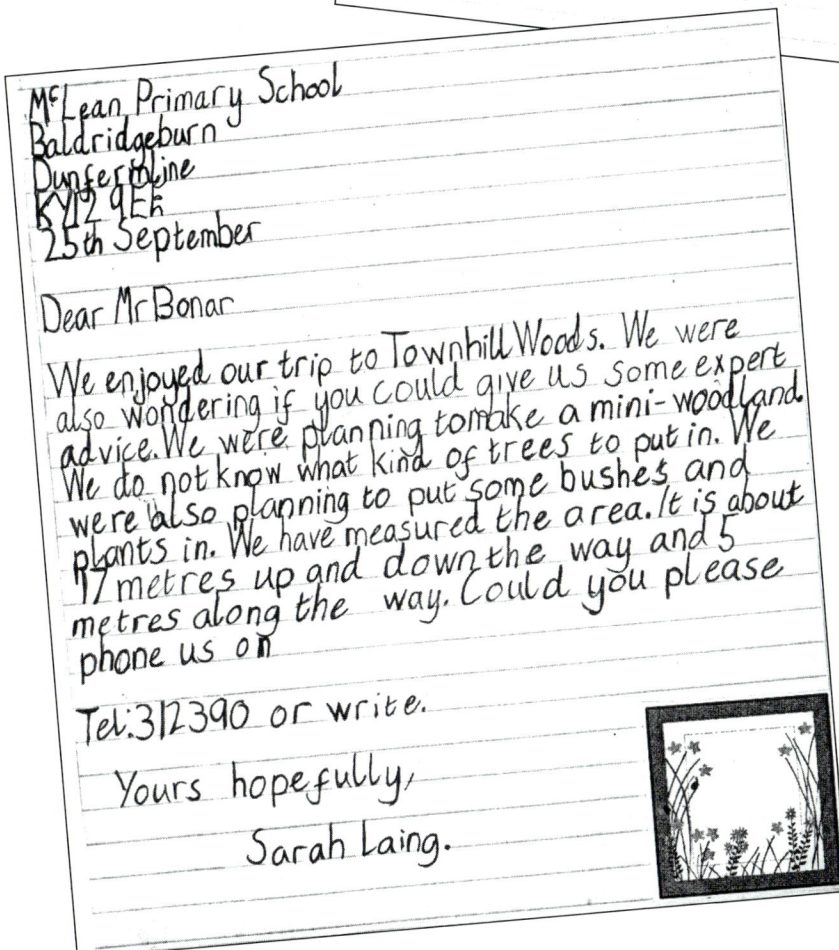

Rebecca Watt
McLean Primary School
Baldridgeburn
Dunfermline
KY12 9EE
25th September

Dear Mr. Bonar

We thought you were so good on our trip and so knowledgeable and you knew lots about trees.

We would very much like you to come to McLean Primary School because we are planning on building our own mini woodland in the school ground and we would like you to come and help us to find out which trees to plant.

Could you please contact McLean Primary School by letter or by phone.

Yours hopefully
Rebecca Watt (Mrs Sinclairs Primary 5)

McLean Primary School
Baldridgeburn
Dunfermline
KY12 9EE
25th September

Dear Mr Bonar

We enjoyed our trip to Townhill Woods. We were also wondering if you could give us some expert advice. We were planning to make a mini-woodland. We do not know what kind of trees to put in. We were also planning to put some bushes and plants in. We have measured the area. It is about 17 metres up and down the way and 5 metres along the way. Could you please phone us on

Tel: 312390 or write.

Yours hopefully,

Sarah Laing.

P5 (AGES 8/9)
McLEAN PRIMARY SCHOOL,
DUNFERMLINE, FIFE

ACTIVITY 16A: Pets

SCIENCE LEARNING OUTCOMES

▶ Know that animals are living things.

▶ Know that animals need certain things to stay alive.

▶ Know that there are different kinds of animals.

SCIENCE ACTIVITY

Arrange a visit to a local veterinary surgery or pet shop. Before the visit arrange for a letter to be sent to the children inviting them to come and see where animals are looked after and to learn about different types of animals and how people look after them.

After the visit, when the children are back in the classroom, discuss what they saw and what they learned. Ask them to think about what they would need if they wanted to make a veterinary surgery or a pet shop in their classroom. Make a list and ask children what kind of things they could bring from home to help create the surgery or shop.

Discuss with children the idea of changing the imaginative or role-play area into a vet's surgery or pet shop. With the children, recreate the place they visited inside the classroom. Children can use it for role-play and specific science activities, such as sorting animals into groups or naming animals.

LITERACY LINK

Very young children can develop the concept that print conveys meaning through writing and receiving letters. Read a letter sent by a friendly pet shop owner or vet, or one written by yourself, to the children and talk about what it says and how it is organised: address, Dear..., message, sender's name.

Create a template of a letter which can be duplicated or placed on a computer for children to complete. They might use drawings or a computer concept keyboard to create their letter. For example:

Dear Vet,

I have a

[puppy/hamster/rabbit/cat]

It has a poorly

[ear/leg/eye/foot]

I feed it on

[seed/grass/fish/carrots/tins of food]

Please tell me what to do to make it better.

From

[child types name]

Letters

ACTIVITY 16B: Decay

SCIENCE LEARNING OUTCOMES

▶ Know that some materials decay and others do not.

▶ Know that some materials are biodegradable.

▶ Understand that litter has a negative effect on the environment.

SCIENCE ACTIVITY

Children who have had experience of sorting, classifying and testing a range of materials notice that the problem of litter is increasing around the outside of their school. Much of the litter is also blowing into the school grounds. They decide to put a case together in the hope of persuading their local authority to take action.

The children carry out the following activities:

▶ **Bury a clean selection of typical waste littering the surrounding area in an unused corner of the school grounds to find out which materials will decompose over time.**

⚠️ **SAFETY.** Children should not collect and bury 'real litter'. Provide 'clean litter', such as packages and tins, for them. See the ASE booklet *Be safe!* for further information.

▶ **After six weeks, dig up the labelled litter items and record the findings.**

▶ **During the same period children keep a log of the type and amount of litter outside the school and inside the school grounds.**

Having collected their evidence the children decide to write to their local authority and explain the problem, providing their evidence in a report and offering a set of suggestions for action.

LITERACY LINK

It is important when children write letters that they have a reason for writing and an audience. In this case the audience is the local authority and children have to consider the following:

▶ Who is the audience?

▶ Do we need to tell them why we are writing to them?

▶ What do we want to tell them?

▶ What do they need to know?

▶ Which parts of our investigation should we tell them?

▶ How can we convince them that our evidence is reliable?

▶ What should our report look like?

▶ What do we want them to do?

▶ What response would we like to our letter?

Encourage children to think about the presentation of their letter and report. Allow them to word-process their work and to use headed paper, if appropriate. Children should also go through a drafting and redrafting process where they check their own work.

TOPIC 17 ▶ OFFICIAL REPORTS AND CONSUMER INFORMATION

KEY ISSUES

▶ Children should be able to access official reports and consumer information.

▶ Children should have some opportunities to question the validity of the data in official reports and consumer information.

▶ Both types of material should be subject to scrutiny and question by children. Children should develop an appreciation that some reports and consumer information may be biased and only offer a certain point of view.

▶ The type of material that could be offered to children might include health advice, material from the local garden centre and *'Which?'* type consumer information.

▶ Children should discuss the characteristics of this type of material:

• *What style of writing is used?*

• *How does it present different types of information?*

• *How many different ways of presenting information are used – prose, lists, diagrams, cartoons, tables, graphs?*

▶ A wide range of this kind of material should be offered to children, increasing in complexity, amount and type of information offered, over the primary years.

▶ The teacher should discuss with children what the purpose of this type of written material is and make a list to help them when they create their own.

SUPPORTING STRATEGIES

▶ Collect and display a range of official reports and consumer information, such as leaflets from dentist, vet, doctor, garden centre, environmental groups.

▶ Cut up leaflets and place them in boxes or under headings according to the purpose of the paragraph, heading, and so on. For example, classify parts of a leaflet under the following headings:

• *Headline*

• *Introduction*

• *Key information*

• *Key words*

• *Instructions*

• *Addresses*

• *Key points*

• *Further information*

▶ Encourage children to use the headings to create their own leaflets and reports.

▶ Before children begin creating their own leaflet or report ask them to consider:

• *Who is the report for?*

• *What do they want to know?*

• *What do we want to tell them?*

• *Do we need to add pictures, graphs?*

• *What is our message or messages?*

• *How long should the report be?*

• *What is the most important information we need to include?*

• *How will we make the leaflet attractive and eye catching?*

• *Will it need sections and a contents page?*

Children's work

Children can be offered consumer information and official reports from a wide range of sources on which to base their own writing, e.g. local electricity companies, health authorities. In this example, consumer information from a seed packet has provided the stimulus.

Y4, CLEADON JUNIOR SCHOOL, TYNESIDE. (EXAMPLE TAKEN FROM FEASEY, R. AND SIRAJ-BLATCHFORD, J. (1998) *KEY SKILLS: COMMUNICATION IN SCIENCE*. UNIVERSITY OF DURHAM AND TYNESIDE TEC.)

Instructions For sowing seeds
1. Check that you have got the following things
Plant pot
seeds
compost or soil
water
light
saucer.
2. You need to pour the compost or soil half way up the plant pot. Then you put the seed on your finger and put your finger a little bit in the compost or soil then let go of the seed then cover it with the compost or soil.
Then water the soil or compost and put it on the window sill and wait for about a week and you will see that your plant will be growing. But you still need to water your plant need to turn your plant around when the sun turns around.

Make sure your plant has the following conditions to grow properly
air
water
sunlight/heat light

5000422 116940

surprise seeds

cleadon seeds

49p

Best Before 8/10/00

ACTIVITY 17A: Growing plants from seed

SCIENCE LEARNING OUTCOMES

▶ Know that different seeds grow into different kinds of plants.

▶ Know that plants need certain things to grow.

▶ Be able to grow plants.

SCIENCE ACTIVITY

Growing plants from seeds is a common activity for children of this age. Allow children to plant their own seeds and record the following information which can be used at a later date to support a linked Literacy Hour:

▶ drawing of the seeds;

▶ explanation of how the seeds were planted;

▶ where the seeds were kept;

▶ amount and number of times the seeds were watered;

▶ photographic or drawn account to show the different stages of growth;

▶ record of regular measurements of the plants.

Children could record the information using a 'Plant Diary' in the form of a mini-book or a strip cartoon.

LITERACY LINK–LITERACY HOUR

For this Literacy Hour activity children will need one or more seed packets with information on them about the seeds and instructions on how to germinate the seeds and grow the plant successfully.

SHARED TEXT WORK (15 MINS)
Create a large 'seed packet' with instructions on a white board or large sheet of paper, or photocopy a seed packet on to an OHP acetate so that all the children can read the information on it. Read and discuss the type of information on the packet with the children. Talk about any new words, such as *germinate*. Make a list of the different types of information on the seed packet for future use and reference.

FOCUSED WORD AND SENTENCE WORK (15 MINS)
Using one of the plants the children have grown as an example, create a 'class seed packet' (extra large version for all of the children to see) and negotiate the information to go on it, where it should be placed, the correct form of words, and so on.

INDEPENDENT WRITING (20 MINS)
Ask children to draft seed packet information for the plants they have grown that will help someone else to plant and grow the same seeds.

WHOLE-CLASS REVIEW (10 MINS)
Share children's work, commenting on examples of different aspects of the seed packets to ensure that as many children receive feedback on their seed packet as possible.

Official reports and consumer information ▶ ACTIVITY 17B: Flammability

SCIENCE LEARNING OUTCOMES

▶ Know that heating materials can cause changes.
▶ Know that the changes caused by heating a material are usually not reversible.
▶ Understand that different materials burn at different rates and some give off noxious fumes.

SCIENCE ACTIVITY

⚠️ This activity has safety implications because children will be using a naked flame and burning small samples of fabric. Before carrying out the activity, refer to the ASE booklet, *Be safe! Some aspects of safety in school science and technology for key stages 1 and 2*, for appropriate safety precautions.

Provide children with information leaflets on safety in the home from their local fire department or the Royal Society for the Prevention of Accidents. Discuss safety in the home in relation to fire, for example:

▶ flammable materials, e.g. soft furnishing, clothing;

▶ use of smoke alarms;

▶ how to make homes safer;

▶ dos and don'ts in the home.

Set the children the problem of helping a responsible furniture manufacturer to choose the best fabric for chair coverings. Ask the children to consider what they think 'best' means in this context; for example, is it a fabric that, when burning:

▶ gives off no or limited fumes?

▶ produces no smoke?

▶ produces no flames?

▶ is slow burning?

Challenge children to plan and carry out an investigation to find out which fabric is best for household furniture. Before they carry out their investigation check that they have developed an appropriate set of safety rules for carrying out the activity.

Ask children to explain what kinds of observations and records they will make. Will they be a mixture of measurements, such as how long the fabric takes to burn, and more qualitative observations such as whether it produces flames, gives off fumes or smoke.

LITERACY LINK

Children can use their knowledge of safety in the home and the results of their investigation to create a report for the furniture manufacturer and a leaflet about safety in the home. They will need to consider:

▶ the audience – who will read the material?

▶ how to convince the audience that their results are valid;

▶ how to make the report or leaflet interesting as well as informative;

▶ what information is vital;

▶ what other material could be included, e.g. pictures, diagrams, puzzles.

Children should draft, review and edit their report or leaflet using knowledge of similar material. Once the draft is complete they should have the opportunity to redraft to publication standard and use ICT to create the finished product.

TOPIC 18　BIOGRAPHICAL AND AUTOBIOGRAPHICAL WRITING

KEY ISSUES

▶ Offering children 'stories' about people in science gives them an opportunity to develop an understanding that science has a 'human face' and that science is as much about people as it is facts and phenomena.

▶ Careful choice of 'people' can help to raise a range of issues in science, for example gender and racism, indicating that science is not always value-free and that it is important that all people have access to science.

▶ Important attitudes can be developed; for example, respecting people regardless of race, gender, class, ability or disability.

▶ Children can develop an appreciation that science involves people who have exciting and interesting stories to tell.

▶ Books and other material available in school should be checked to ensure that children have access to a range of people involved in science, women as well as men, and scientists from different countries and cultures.

SUPPORTING STRATEGIES

▶ Create a 'Scientist of the Month' display board on which stories, posters and information about a scientist and their invention or field of work can be displayed and celebrated. Include ways in which the work of the scientist has influenced life today.

▶ Offer children the opportunity to role-play the story of the scientist; for example, to write, produce and perform a play.

▶ Offer children contemporary scientists as well as scientists from history.

▶ Biographies and autobiographies can be written using different forms of writing; for example, plays, poems, strip cartoons, prose, role-play which is video-taped.

▶ Invite a scientist into the classroom for children to interview. Encourage children to ask questions about their everyday life as well as their work in science. This helps children to appreciate that scientists are people too and often have families, favourite sports, and so on. Encourage children to make notes, or alternatively video or tape-record the interview, so that they can access the information as a resource. Children could use their notes to write a biography of the person.

▶ On page 111 is the story of Charles Drew who developed blood transfusion. This story could be used with children to create, for example, newspaper articles or a role-play interview.

Biographical and autobiographical writing

Children's work

There are many interesting people in science, in the past and the present. Children can research biographical details and write about individuals in different ways. Here children have been learning about Charles Drew.

The story of Charles Drew is a tragic one; he died because doctors refused to give him blood because he was black. Ironically it was Charles Drew who was behind the development of blood transfusions. The story of Charles Drew is available for children to read on page 111 of the Resources section.

DAILY STAR

Tragic Death Without Blood

By David Preece

01/02/98 11:08:24

Charles Drew before he died

Today's element to the news is appalling.
A man was dragged into hospital and badly needed blood, but the doctors and nurses refused. The man whose name was Charles Drew was a scientist who discoverd the blood transfusion who died after nurses did not give him any blood.

The lawyers {above} are simply appalled about this news.

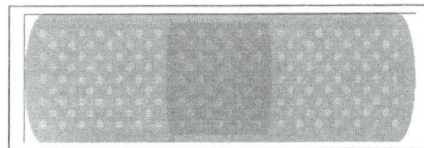

Give blood and be happy

Y5, ST THOMAS MORE RC PRIMARY SCHOOL, DURHAM

ACTIVITY 18A: Scientists

SCIENCE LEARNING OUTCOMES

▶ Know about different scientists.

▶ Know that children can think and work like scientists.

SCIENCE ACTIVITY

It is important that children know that they are engaged in science, just as they know that they are doing mathematics, English, history, art, PE or any curriculum subject. Talking about scientists and the way they work allows children to appreciate the parallels with the way they themselves work in science. For example, scientists:

▶ use special equipment;

▶ use tables;

▶ think about what will happen;

▶ ask and answer questions;

▶ carry out fair tests.

By discussing a scientist, whether one from history or a parent or friend of the school whom they have interviewed, children begin to understand what it means to be a scientist.

Ask children to consider what they think a scientist is like and what a scientist does. Offer them a two-column table into which they brainstorm a list of words and phrases linked to scientists and themselves when they do science in the classroom. For example:

What scientists do and think about	What we do and think about in our science lessons
use equipment	we measure things
measure	we use equipment
predict	we make sure our tests are fair
carry out a fair test	
use a table	
make a graph	

Talk to children about the link between themselves and scientists, encouraging them to think of themselves as scientists and that when they do their science they are doing something special, interesting and exciting.

LITERACY LINK

Although biographies and autobiographies are not a feature of literacy work at this level, children could be offered several tasks related to this activity which help to develop a range of literacy skills, as well as introducing children to the idea that some books tell the story of a person.

Read or tell children a story about a famous scientist and ask them to re-tell the story of that person, for example as role-play or a 'story'. Children could also write about themselves as a scientist, for example:

I am a scientist when I do science in my class. These are some of the things I think about and do...

Create with the children a book about famous scientists. Children are expected to know about famous authors of fiction and names of famous artists so it is equally appropriate for them to begin to appreciate that there are famous scientists. Include in the book scientists in history as well as some scientists from their community and, of course, the children themselves. They might offer a picture of themselves and information about which aspects of science particularly interest them. For example:

My name is Peter and I am a scientist at school. I really like doing work on magnets.

Biographical and autobiographical writing ACTIVITY 18B: The human body – blood

SCIENCE LEARNING OUTCOMES

▶ Know that the heart is a major organ.

▶ Know that the heart pumps blood around the body.

▶ Understand what blood does and its importance in the body.

SCIENCE ACTIVITY

Children do not always realise that blood is central to life and does many jobs in our body every minute of the day. Providing children with some basic information about blood, such as that below, and asking them to carry out some simple activities can help them to appreciate how vital blood is to life.

▶ The heart beats approximately 70 times a minute.

▶ Each time the heart beats 117 ml of blood is pumped from the heart.

▶ Blood carries oxygen around the body.

▶ Blood carries nutrients from the digestive system to all parts of the body.

▶ Blood has special cells that help the body to fight disease.

▶ Blood clots when the skin is broken.

▶ Blood takes waste products from the body to the kidneys.

Ask children to calculate:

▶ the number of beats their heart has made since they were born;

▶ how much blood is pumped from the heart in one minute;

▶ how many litres of blood that amounts to.

Children could write to the Blood Transfusion Service to find out more information about blood and how the service works today.

LITERACY LINK–LITERACY HOUR

The story of Charles Drew on page 111 provides the basis for this Literacy Hour activity.

SHARED TEXT WORK (15 MINS)
Read with children the story of Charles Drew and discuss the idea that it is a biography because someone has written about him. Talk about some of the main issues raised by the story. For example:

▶ Charles Drew died because he was denied the very thing he developed;

▶ attitudes of people in the southern states of America during that period;

▶ how they think Charles Drew would have felt if he had survived.

FOCUSED WORD AND SENTENCE WORK (15 MINS)
Discuss with the children what kind of changes would have to be made if they were to change the story from a biography into an autobiography. Encourage them to think about what kind of words they would use in an autobiography. Challenge children to change sentences to make them read as though it is Charles Drew's autobiography. Compare and discuss the sentences and encourage children to take on the role of 'critical friend' and offer constructive comments to their friends.

INDEPENDENT WRITING (20 MINS)
During this period the children can begin to rewrite material as an autobiography, taking the role of Charles Drew describing his research and how he was refused access to a blood transfusion. Encourage children to describe emotions as well as facts relating to the story.

WHOLE-CLASS REVIEW (10 MINS)
Ask individuals to read their autobiography aloud and invite comment from the rest of the class.

References and further reading

Ahlberg, A. and Ahlberg, J. (1982) *Funny Bones.* London: Collins.

ASE (1990) *Be safe! Some aspects of safety in school science and technology for key stages 1 and 2.* 2nd edn. Hatfield, Herts: Association for Science Education.

ASE (1998) *Science Education for the Year 2000 and Beyond.* Hatfield, Herts: Association for Science Education.

Bearne, E. ed. (1998) *Use of language across the primary curriculum.* London: Routledge.

Burningham, J. *Mr Gumpy's Motor Car.* London: Penguin.

DfEE (1998) *The National Literacy Strategy.* DfEE Publications.

Driver, R., Leach, J. and Scott, P. (1996) *Young people's images of science.* Buckingham: Open University Press.

Feasey, R. and Siraj-Blatchford, J. (1998) *Key skills: Communication in science.* University of Durham/Tyneside Training and Enterprise Council.

Lewis, M. and Wray, D. (1995) *Developing children's non-fiction writing: Working with writing frames.* Leamington Spa: Scholastic.

Lewis, M. and Wray, D. (1997) *Extending literacy: Children reading and writing non-fiction.* London: Routledge.

Littlefair, A. (1991) *Reading all kinds of writing.* Buckingham: Open University Press.

Mallet, M. (1992) *Making facts matter: Reading non-fiction 5–11.* London: Paul Chapman.

Meek, M. (1996) *Information and book learning.* Stroud: Thimble Press.

Neate, B. (1992) *Finding out about finding out.* Sevenoaks: Hodder and Stoughton.

Reid, D. and Bentley, D. ed. (1996) *Reading on! Developing reading at key stage 2.* Leamington Spa: Scholastic.

Photocopiable resources

The following section offers a range of material for use with children either in Literacy Hours or during science sessions. The material can be photocopied and used, for example, with individuals, with small groups, or as OHP acetates for use with the whole class.

Topic 1: Oral re-telling of science experiences
Topic 5: Sequencing events

LINK Topic 2: Labels and captions

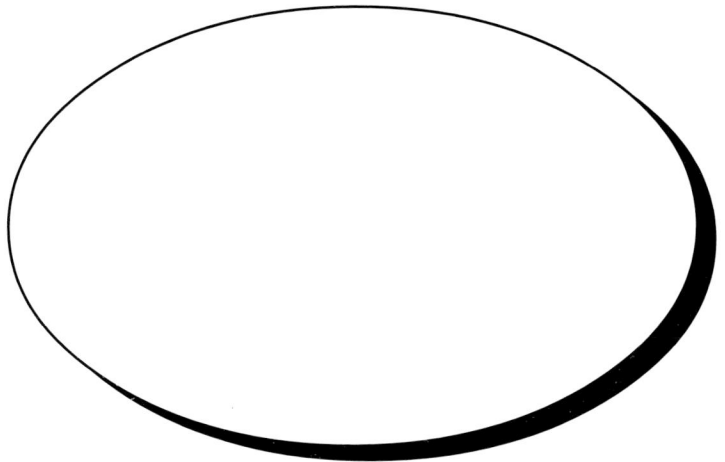

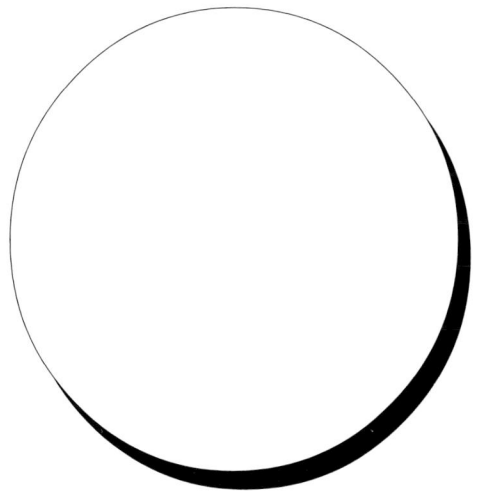

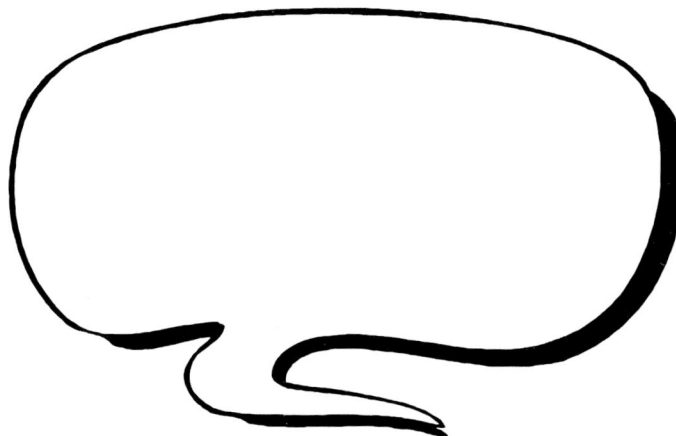

LINK ▶ Topic 3: Scientific vocabulary   **Key stage 1 science words**

Exploration and investigations

accurate
ask
carry out
chart
compare
decide
explain
fair
find out
group
guess
how
investigate
measure
observe
plan
question
sort
table
test
why

Environment
alive
animal
camouflage
compost
differences
environment
farm
field
garden
grass
habitat
hedge
home
insects
litter
living
plant
pollution
pond
seashore
sort
underground
wild
woodland

Light

beam
block
bright
bulb
camera
candle
colour
dark
electricity
eye
fire
flame
glasses
kaleidoscope
lens
light
look
mirror
opaque
photograph
picture
prism
rainbow
ray
reflect
reflection
see
shade
shadow
star
sun
telescope
torch
transparent

Forces
bend
bounce
change
down
drop
further
height
move
pull
push
pushing back
roll
rough

smooth
squash
steep
stretch
turn
twist
up

Electricity
battery
bulb
circuit
conductor
current
flex
heat
hot
insulator
lamp
light
motor
movement
off
on
plug
power station
pylon
safety
shock
sound
spark
static
switch
wire

Magnets
attract
bar
compass
force
fridge magnet
horse-shoe
iron filings
iron
magnetic
non-magnetic
north
pole
pull
push

repel
south

Ourselves and other animals
adult
alive
animal
arm
baby
bacteria
bird
blood
body
breathe
bud
bulb
camouflage
child
dead
drugs
ears
egg
eyes
feed
feet
fish
fly
food
fur
gills
grow
hair
hands
hear
heart
human
insect
lungs
move
plant
scales
senses
skeleton
short
swim
tall
walk

Materials
absorb
air

bend
clay
cold
different
dissolve
dough
dry
dull
fabric
fibre
freeze
glass
grains
group
heat
heavy
hot
lamp
liquid
magnetic
melt
metal
mixture
mould
opaque
plastic
Plasticine
rock
rough
sand
separate
sharp
shiny
similar
smooth
soak
soft
solid
sort
squashy
stretchy
strong
temperature
texture
thick
thin
translucent
transparent
twist
water
weight
wet
wood
wool

LINK ▷ Topic 3: Scientific vocabulary   Key stage 2 science words

Exploration and investigations
approximate
average
believable
best fit
change
classify
compare
conclusion
contrast
control
describe
diagram
effects
evaluate
experiment
fair test
graph
group
investigation
label
learned
maximum
measure
method
minimum
observe
pattern
plan
predict
reading
reliable
repeat
resources
results
sort
table
units

Environment
adaptation
amphibian
anther
artery
bacteria
carnivore
classification
consumer
decay

digestion
ecosystem
energy
environment
fertilisation
food chains
food webs
herbivore
mammal
minerals
omnivore
plant
photosynthesis
poison
pollen
pollination
pollution
predator
prey
producer
recycle
reproduction
reptile
rot
stamen
stigma
survival
variation

Light
angle
develop
energy
lens
light-emitting
    diode (LED)
optical
primary source
secondary source
translucent

Forces
attraction
balance
displacement
Earth
force
friction
gravity

magnetic force
mass
movement
Newton
repulsion
rotate
slope
support
surface
time
weight

Electricity
cell
connector
diagram
parallel
series
short-circuit

Magnets
electromagnet
field
magnetised

Ourselves and other animals
arteries
blood
brain
diet
food chain
heart
kidneys
life-cycle
liver
living
lungs
movement
muscles
non-living
nutrition
organs
pulse
sensitivity
skeleton
veins
weight

Materials
absorbent
attract
burn
carbon dioxide
Celsius
chemical
condense
conductor
degrees
dissolve
density
evaporate
evaporation
fabric
filter
flammable
flexible
fluid
gases
insoluble
insulator
irreversible
manufactured
mass
natural
opaque
properties
repel
reversible
solution
translucent
volume

What happens to the food that you eat?

Answer this question using some or all of the following words:

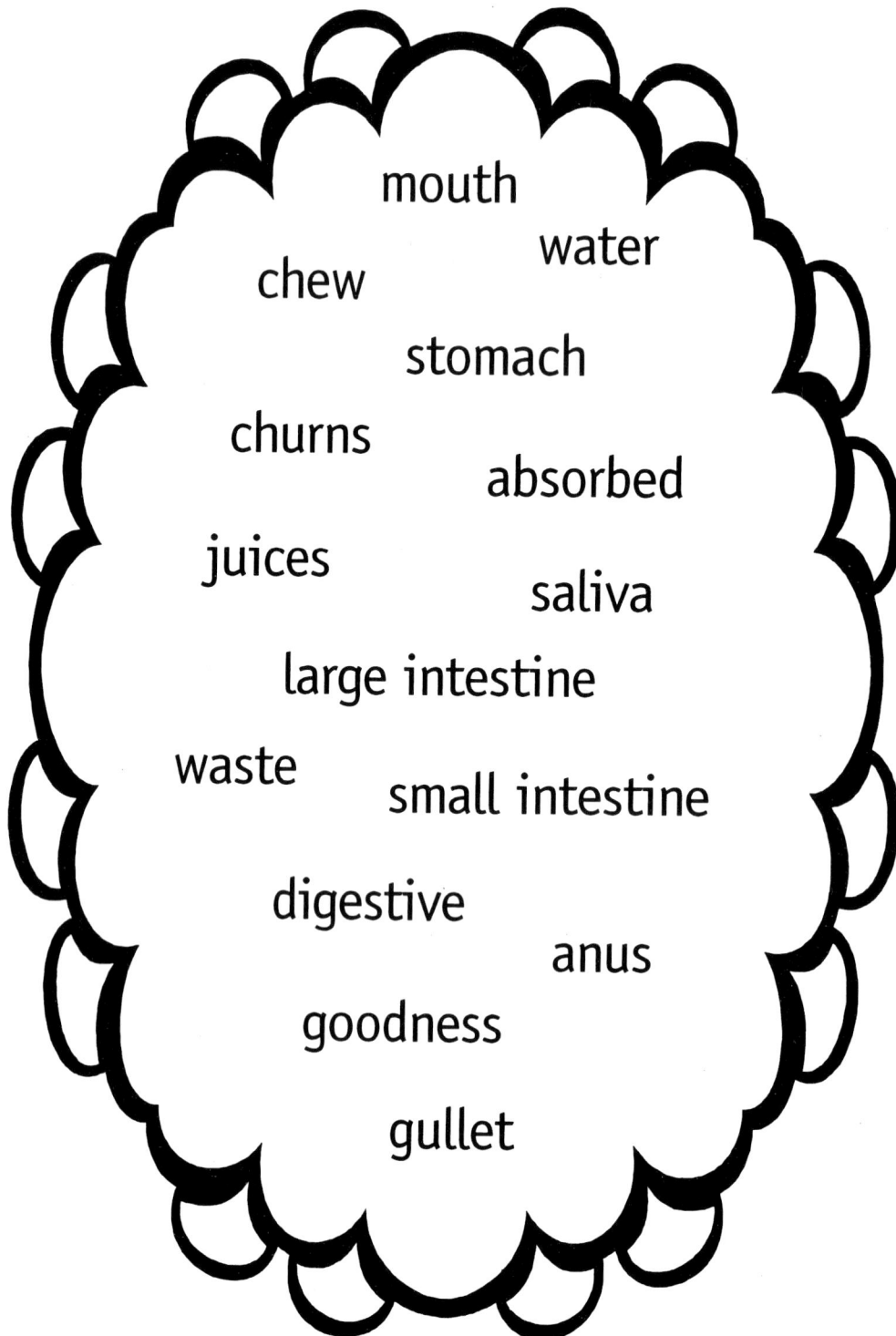

mouth

water

chew

stomach

churns

absorbed

juices

saliva

large intestine

waste

small intestine

digestive

anus

goodness

gullet

Please write a draft copy first!   Isis CE Primary School, Oxford

| LINK ▶ Topic 3: Scientific vocabulary | | | | Prefixes |

Prefix	Words	What do you think it means?	Dictionary definition	Marks out of 10 for your own definition
Aero – air	aerobic aeroplane aerate aerodynamic			
Anti – against	antiseptic anti-toxins			
Bi – two	binary biceps biennial			
Bio – life	biodegradable biodiversity biology biomass biosphere biotechnology			
Chloro – green	chlorophyll chloroplasts			
Chromo – colour	chromatography			
Photo – light	photosynthesis phototropism			

Now think of other prefixes in science and words that contain them. Create your own Prefix Table.

LINK ▷ Topic 4: Dictionaries and glossaries

A–Z of the Body

A . . . .   N . . . .

B . . . .   O . . . .

C . . . .   P . . . .

D . . . .   Q . . . .

E . . . .   R . . . .

F . . . .   S . . . .

G . . . .   T . . . .

H . . . .   U . . . .

I . . . .   V . . . .

J . . . .   W . . . .

K . . . .   X . . . .

L . . . .   Y . . . .

M . . . .   Z . . . .

Glossary – Earth and Space

asteroid . . . .

astronomer . . . .

comet . . . .

constellation . . . .

crater . . . .

galaxy . . . .

meteorite . . . .

moon . . . .

observatory . . . .

planet . . . .

star . . . .

telescope . . . .

LINK ▶ Topic 5: Sequencing events   **Scrambled eggs**

What you will need

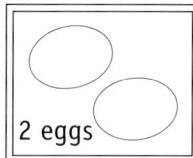

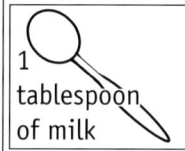

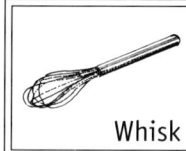

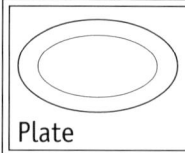

2 eggs

1 tablespoon of milk

Mixing bowl

Whisk

Small knob of butter

Saucepan

Plate

Knife & Fork

Wooden spoon

Break eggs into bowl

Add milk

Whisk milk and eggs together

⚠ **An adult must do this part**

Melt butter in pan

⚠ **An adult must do this part**

Pour mixture into pan. Stir until cooked

Eat the scrambled eggs

My INVESTIGATION
BY
....

Here is a picture of
what we did.

This is how we
kept it fair...

This is what
happened...

Was I right?

Our question is...

This is the answer to our question...

This is what I think will happen...

LINK ▶ Topic 6: Using tenses, verbs, adjectives, etc.

The Journey of a Coke can

I'm plundging towards a huge plastic gaping hole. It's all dark. Just a few minutes ago I was being emptied into a giant's mouth. After all ive done this is what I get for it. I have to be next a bannana peel, I mean talk about punishment. He is so dopey. After trying to think positivly after what might happen. I felt myself being jolted up and down, I was moving! It smelt, I was thrown into a huge box, well I don't how big it was. I was tied up in some huge sack. For ages I bumped about and it was like an earthquake. I jumped at the end when we must have stopped. It was then that I felt myself floating in mid-air. I was petrified. Then I got hurled at a wall. It was like a cliff face. I was squeezed against a toilet roll. He was just snooty. This was much more of a smooth ride even though we were packed together like sardines. The way people treat us it's as if we don't matter. It went all bright then and I could just make out a mountain of soil and all by old freinds. I wonder if thats im going to. I think were going up hill ive just moved down into a cork from a Wine bottle. He keeps muttering something I think he's had one too many. ow! I just hit the side. I can hear a creaking, it must be the door of the lorry. Where am I? All I can see is a world in the middle of nowhere covered in rubbish and waste. I'm falling down and down and down... I thought I was going to hit the ground but I just hit more rubbish. Theres an endless shower of bottles, packets, bags, everything. After about a day all I could see was rubbish and we were so squashed together I couldn't move. It was then that I heard something and it went all dark. We must of been covered up.

by Fizzy.

LINK Topic 7: Using openers and connectives

Beginning

Our question asks us....

We started with...

Our problem is...

To answer the question we need...

To begin with we will....

I am going to explain how...

We will investigate...

What we already know

We already know that...

Before we began we did some research...

We think ... because...

We know that ... because...

When we have tried this before....

Tables and graphs

The pattern suggests...

The result for .... was unexpected. It could be because...

Another reason for the results could be...

We were surprised...

We think that the graph shows that....

The graphs looks like this because...

There is a link between...

Conclusions

This proves...

This explains why...

Our results are different to what we thought would happen because...

The results show that....

Looking at the results it seems likely that...

Our evidence suggests that...

We concluded that....

We think that....

Using our results we can say that...

LINK Topic 8: Asking questions

10 Questions

Who? What? Could? How? If? Would?

How? Will? Do? Did?

Where? Should?

What if? Can? Have? When?

1

2

3

4

5

6

7

8

9

10

12 QUESTIONS

Venus

1	What is the mass of Venus?
2	Where would we make our homes on Venus?
3	Who discovered Venus and when?
4	Why did they call this planet "Venus"?
5	Is there water on Venus? If so, where?
6	Will we ever live on Venus? If so when?
7	If we lived on Venus what would happen?
8	Where is Venus in the Solar System?
9	Would the solar system be different without Venus?
10	Have people ever tried to get to Venus in history? If so who?
11	What is the force of Gravity on Venus compared to earth?
12	How could we survive on Venus?

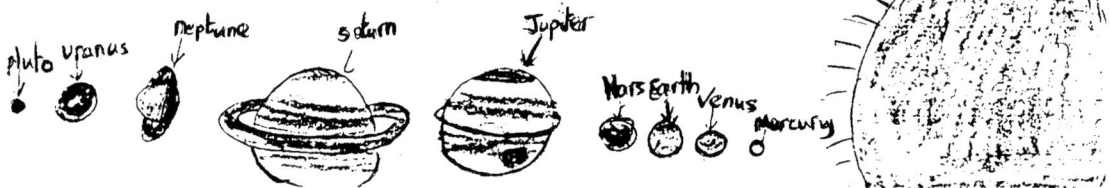

N. ARMSTRONG

sun
Pluto Uranus neptune saturn Jupiter Mars Earth Venus Mercury

LINK Topic 9: Answering questions

10 Answers

1	
2	
3	
4	
5	
6	
7	
8	
9	
10	

LINK ▶ Topic 9: Answering questions

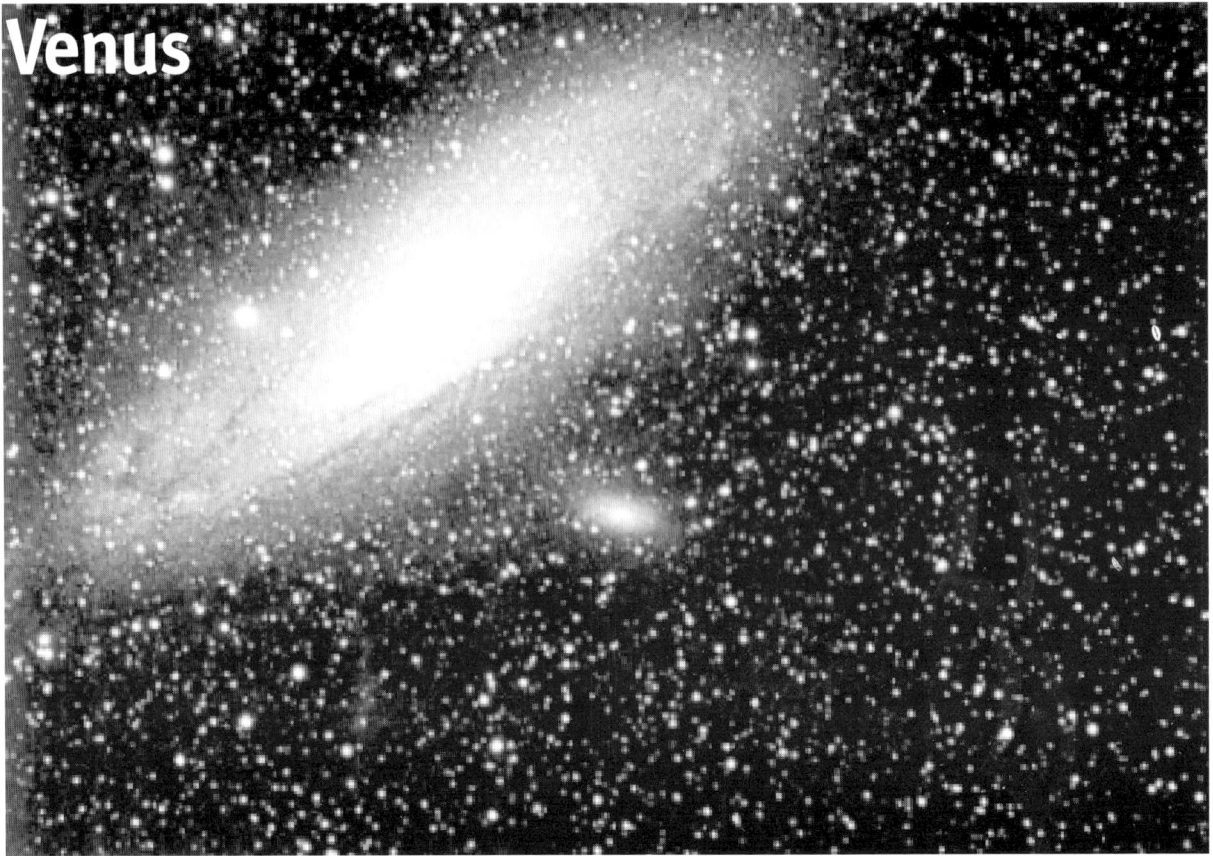

Venus

Venus is the second planet from the Sun and because of this the surface temperature of this planet is approximately 462 °C. Its diameter is 12,103 km (7521 miles) and it was discovered by Galileo.

The atmosphere of this planet is different from Earth's, since not only is it hotter but the surface pressure is 96 times that on Earth. The composition is also different. It consists of nearly all carbon dioxide with clouds that are made up of sulphuric acid. It is an inhospitable place and it is unlikely that humans would ever be able to live there because of the intense heat and poisonous clouds.

Venus is also known as the Morning or Evening Star because it can be seen in the east at sunrise and in the west at sunset. It is 108 million kilometres from the Sun, takes 225 days to orbit the Sun and spins backwards.

Humans have tried to study Venus but because of the cloud cover this is not easy. However, the *Mariner* spacecrafts launched by the United States and the *Venera* crafts sent by the Soviet Union have provided information about this planet. More recently the *Magellan* probe has sent back images of the planet.

LINK ▶ Topic 10: Poetry   1

Sadness

Fighting for life,
Fighting for air
Drugs, operations were
done.
So still in a hospital

Grandad laid
Unaware what was happening.
A glance I took
I was helpless, destroyed,
Sadness strings broke free

And flooded my body
But the lump blocked my throat.
I just stood there.
All the happy times floated
through my mind.

Karleigh Homeward, Y6, WERRINGTON PRIMARY SCHOOL CAMBRIDGESHIRE

Five Ages

As a baby so tiny, cute, fragile and dependent,

You learn to walk and talk and become so demanding,

You're active, more talkative and capable,

When you reach the Juniors.

When you become a teenager you're difficult

And you think you're the best.

You're moody and covered in spots.

Clothes are important

Hair has to be just right.

But when you're an adult you have to be sensible,

Get a job, clean the house and look after the children.

You gradually grow old

Get a wrinkled face and grey hair.

You get your pension money every week

Have time to spare but nothing to do

But think back on the happy times long ago.

Jodie Talbot
Y6, WERRINGTON PRIMARY SCHOOL CAMBRIDGESHIRE

The Living Life of Plants

The ovary gently cradles the seeds,

The stigma softly gathers the pollen,

Gentle filament holds up the attractive anther

The soft breeze delicately blows the yellow anther

The fragile stalk rocks the flower.

Colourful petals attract all.

Debra, Rachel and Hollie
GRANGE PARK PRIMARY SCHOOL, SUNDERLAND

LINK ▶ Topic 10: Poetry   2

Dark Planet

Black and dark, bitter and
cold.
The rocky core as thick as
gold.
It has no company except
the stars.
No noisy inventions like
lorries or cars.
Methane clouds wrap
around the planet like
cotton wool.
They form a shadow to
make it dull.
One of the three planets
furthest from the Sun.
If there had been a prize
for the dullest planet it
surely would have won.

Kate Masters
ST THOMAS MORE RC PRIMARY
SCHOOL, DURHAM

Pluto

Pluto is Dark
Cloudy
Dull
Overcast
Grey
Gloomy

Pluto is Cold
Freezing
Icy
Frosty
Chilly
Raw

Pluto is Small
Tiny
Tiny-Weeny
Microscopic

Nathaniel
ST THOMAS MORE RC PRIMARY
SCHOOL, DURHAM

In the Blackness of the Sky

In the Blackness of the Sky
Stars twinkling
Comets flying
Moons shining
Mars spinning
Blackholes killing
Venus burning
Saturn glowing
Uranus floating
Milky Way disappearing
Galaxies relaxing
Asteroids shooting
Rockets whizzing
Space station refuelling
In the blackness of the sky.

All of year 6
ST THOMAS MORE RC PRIMARY SCHOOL,
DURHAM

The Candle

**Poems written after children had observed an
unlit candle which was then lit and blown out.
At each stage the children wrote down their
observations and extended these through
drafting to produce the poems.**

The wick was white.
The candle was very white.
It looked as if the candle had
never been lit before.
The candle was thin, so very thin,
cylinder in shape at the bottom
but like a cone at the top.
Not for long.
It starts to melt as quick
as tears running down your face.
The cone shape has now gone.
It feels very warm.
The flame has become very big.
Smoke appears.
Now it is blown out.
It is cold again!

Sarah Spencer

The candle is small and cold,
as white as snow, I feel cold.
The candle is lit.
It's a little bit bright.
The flame is yellow.
It smells a bit.
I feel warm.
The wick was white but now it is black.
It is blown out and smoke comes from the
wick.

David Hackford

The flame is flickering.
The wick is getting burnt.
The wax is melting.
The yellow and orange flame burns the wick.
The colours mix together.
I feel warm.
Suddenly the flame goes out
and I go cold.
The smoke smells.

Shaun Baker

Y3, WOLD PRIMARY SCHOOL, HUMBERSIDE

LINK ► Topic 10: Poetry

Chocolate

by Michael Rosen

Look at me, look at me,
I've got chocolate.
It's the end of the party
they've given me chocolate.
Look at me, look at me,
I've got chocolate.
I must keep my chocolate
where no one can get it.
Where shall I put it
in my bag? in my pocket?
No. In my hand. I'll keep it.
Look at me, look at me,
I've got chocolate
and I'm going home to eat
it.

And we walk down the
street,
it's a sunny day and hot
for me and my chocolate
and I've got it, I've got it,
my fingers are round it
tightly closed around it.
Look at me, look at me,
I've got chocolate.

And we get to my house
and I rush in and shout
'Look at me, look at me,
I've got chocolate.'
'Let's see, let's see,
your lovely chocolate...'
And I open up my hands
to show them the
chocolate...
...and oh no!
what do you know!
That lovely big bit

of beautiful chocolate
has gone all soggy
mucky and sticky
like a handful of mud
is all I've got,
is a big sticky mess
oh no, oh yes!

'Look at you, look at you
what are you going to do?'
And I stop and I think
and I think and I stop.
What's in my hand?
What have I really got?
Is it still chocolate?
Is this mess chocolate or not?
I know what
I'll just try a little taste
I take my tongue to my finger

and my finger to my tongue
and YUM!

Look at me, look at me
lick lick lick
chocolate lick
lick it, like it
like it, lick it
sticky, sticky chocolate
lick it and lick it
til there's nothing left
not one little bit.

I've eaten my chocolate.
Look at me.

THIS POEM IS REPRODUCED BY KIND PERMISSION OF MICHAEL ROSEN AND THE STAR* PROJECT.

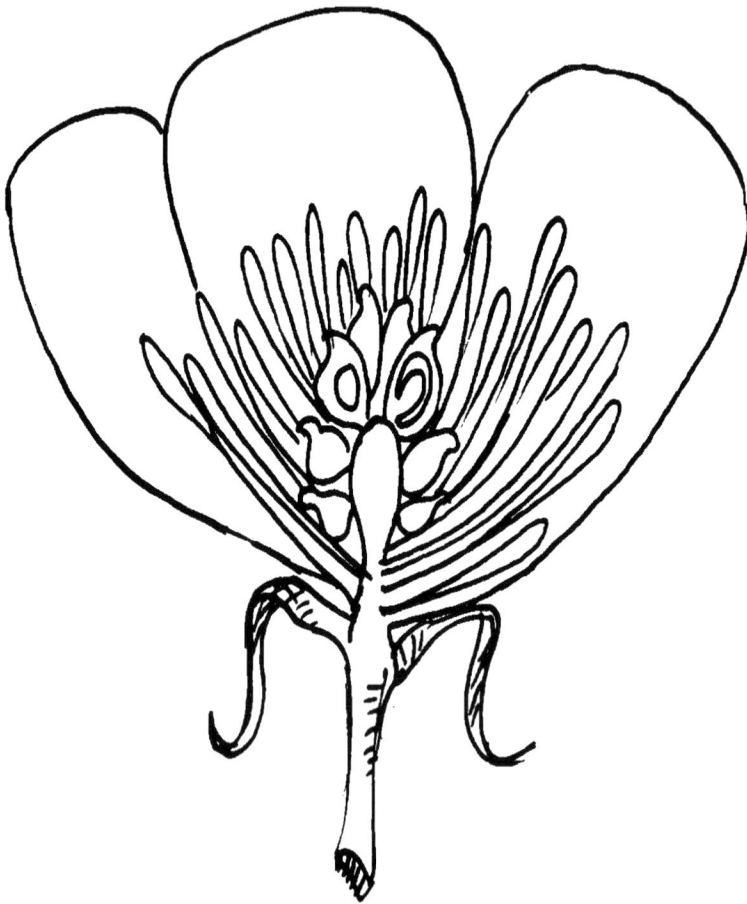

Making notes

When you have read your information, make a list of the key ideas, facts or things that happened.

1	
2	
3	
4	
5	
6	
7	
8	
9	
10	

LINK ▶ Topic 11: Making notes

The heart

The heart is one of the major organs of the body. The heart acts as a pump and keeps blood moving around the body. The heart has two pumps, one on the right side and one on the left. The left one pumps blood which contains oxygen from the heart around the body along the arteries. The blood gives up the oxygen as it travels around the body and the veins take blood back to the right-hand side of the heart.

When the blood gets back to the heart it travels to the lungs to collect more oxygen and begin the process all over again.

Blood flows into and out of the heart, always in the same direction. It never flows backwards. The heart has special valves to stop this from happening. In this way the blood flows around the body. We call this circulation. A heart beats approximately 70 times every minute although this varies from person to person.

Each time the heart beats, approximately 70 ml of blood is forced out of the heart into the arteries. This push from the heart creates something like a wave of blood. In certain places around the body the arteries are close to the skin and the wave can be felt. This is called a pulse. There is a pulse spot at the back of the wrist and at the side of the neck. At these spots you can feel a throbbing sensation. You can count

the number of throbs per minute, which should be the same as the number of heart beats per minute. Counting how many throbs there are in one minute gives you your pulse rate. However, you should not use your thumb to feel because it has a pulse spot of its own.

The heart is a muscle and like other muscles in the body needs exercise. Aerobic exercise means making your heart work a bit harder for a long time. Good aerobic exercises are jogging, cycling, skipping, swimming and walking. When you exercise, your muscles need oxygen. The more you exercise the more oxygen they need, so you breathe in and out more often and the heart has to pump more oxygen around the body. Exercise makes your heart work harder and therefore strengthens your heart. We know that our heart is working harder because our pulse rate goes up.

A heart can become diseased and lead to problems such as high blood pressure and even heart attacks. Lack of exercise and eating too many fatty foods can result in fatty deposits developing inside the arteries which carry blood around the body. These fatty deposits can make the arteries narrow which makes it hard for the blood to pump round the body.

LINK Topic 11: Making notes

The heart

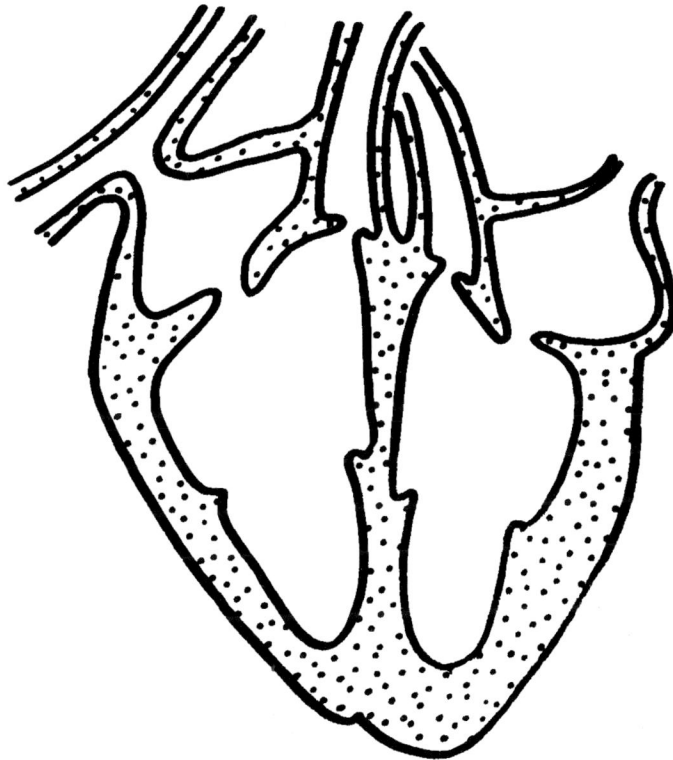

LINK ▷ Topic 12: Instructional text

THOMAS SWAN

SITE SAFETY

All operational areas are dematched. Smoking is only allowed in designated smoking areas.

First Aid treatment for injuries is always available. Your host or appropriate Department Head/Supervisor will act as a contact.

The maximum speed limit on site is 5 mph (8 km/h).

EMERGENCY EVACUATION

In the event of an Emergency the fire alarm (varying pitch notes) will sound continuously. **IMMEDIATELY** go to the security gatehouse for roll call check.

(Note: The alarm system is tested every Friday between 11:30 and 11:45 using bursts of u to ten seconds)

P.T

THOMAS SWAN

DELIVERIES AND COLLECTIONS AND OTHER NON-EMPLOYEES

When on site, adhere to the requirements of the risk assessment and relevant safety rules as detailed by the Thomas Swan Department Head or Supervisor.

CONTRACTORS AND VISITORS ARE REQUESTED TO:

1. Display the badge (issued by security) whilst on site.
2. Return the badge to security on leaving the site.
3. Be escorted by a Thomas Swan employee, or ensure that your whereabouts are known to the appropriate Department Head or Supervisor whilst on site.
4. If working on site, adhere to the requirements of the risk assessment and relevant safety rules as detailed by the Thomas Swan Department Head or Supervisor.

P.T.O

Thomas Swan & Co. Ltd.   Amendment 1: Issued November 1997. Supersedes: Issue 1 / Feb 1996   Doc Ref: 18.1.128

THOMAS SWAN & CO. LTD, CONSETT, CO. DURHAM

LINK ▶ Topic 13: Developing persuasive argument

Persuasive argument

There is a lot of discussion about...

I am going to explain why I think that...

The people who agree with this idea, claim that...

As a result I believe...

They argue that...

So....

A further point is that...

The main reason is...

However there are strong arguments to support this, for example...

I agree because...

After considering the evidence it is obvious that...

I disagree because...

Although not everyone would agree...

You might not agree, but you should consider...

There are several reasons why...

After looking at all of the arguments...

Furthermore...

Some people might argue that...

We would prefer that...

Experience suggests that...

Our evidence shows that...

LINK > Topic 13: Developing persuasive argument

Environmental issues

DAILY HERALD
YOUR MORNING NEWSPAPER • 30P SATURDAY 16 JANUARY 1999

SSSI UNDER THREAT

by C. Hesketh
Environmental
correspondent

YESTERDAY LOCAL PEOPLE attended a public meeting to consider the fate of a Site of Special Scientific Interest.

Brown's Pond, which includes an established pond that can be traced back to the early 1800s and the adjacent marsh area, is part of a proposed development site for a new housing estate and industrial park.

Opinion divided

Opinion at the meeting was clearly divided. Local residents were split into groups, one in favour of the development. Mr Crane from the local Parish Council said: 'Over the years we have lost many people from the village because of the lack of housing and jobs. This development will breathe new life into a village which is in danger of dying.'

Plants and animals will disappear for ever

However, a spokesperson for the local conservation group indicated that the development would have a devastating effect on the local wildlife. Judith Emery said: 'There are at least six species which face extinction if this development goes ahead. The area is an important feeding and breeding ground for many animals, including crested newts and dragonflies, and a stop-over for migrating birds. There is no other similar habitat in the area and once it disappears we will never be able to replace it.'

Emotions were high at the meeting which was the first of a number, and no doubt this debate will continue.

If you want to register you opinion, call OPINION HOTLINE between 9 am and 4 pm any weekday.

LINK	Topic 13: Developing persuasive argument

We are debating...

Arguments for	Arguments against

After considering all of the evidence I think that...

Children Making their own Books in Science 1

A3 book
- Fold an A3 sheet in half, so it's A4.
- Fold in half again, to A5.
- Fold in half again, to A6.
- Open it out like a story board, and fold up again the other way so all the folds will lie flat.
- Open it out.
- Fold like this:
- Cut where shown:

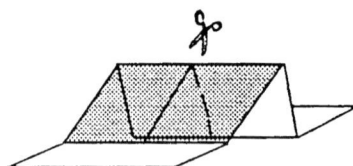

- Open out at the top where you have cut:

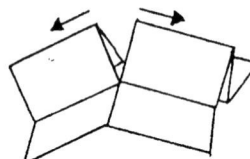

- It should look like this:

- Fold it up to make a book.

Applications: *Anything scientific, or otherwise, plus a way of recording an investigation: Question on the front, Prediction inside, followed by Method, Diagram, Table of results, Graph of results, and Conclusion on following pages.*

Flip book
- Place one piece of A4 paper on top of another of a different colour. Off-set by about a centimetre.

- Fold approximately in half so the resulting book is like this:

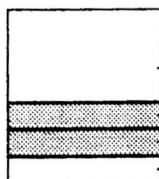

Question and prediction
Method
Results and graph
Conclusion and reason

Our thanks to Lancashire Primary Science Advisory Team for allowing this material to be reproduced.

2

Applications: *Anything scientific, or otherwise, plus a way of recording an investigation (see diagram on previous page), try cutting them into shapes for particular purposes, e.g. a lightbulb shape for a book of light sources.*

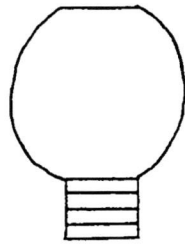

Shutter books

♦   Pinch a fold to mark the centre of an A4 piece of paper:

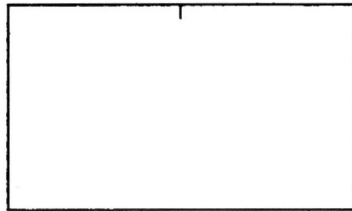

♦   Fold in "shutters" to the pinch mark to make a two shutter book:

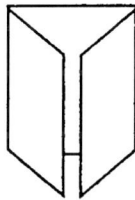

Applications: *Habitats contrasted; Question, method, results, conclusion.*

♦   Fold inwards in half and cut along the folds of the shutters to make a four shutter book.

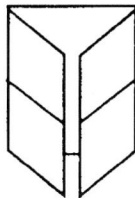

Applications: *Question, method, results, conclusion, one inside each flap.*

LINK	Topic 14: Reading and making science non-fiction books

Cone book   3

- ◆   Cut off the end of an A4 piece of paper to make a square piece.
- ◆   Fold the square across both diagonals, and cut up one diagonal to the centre.

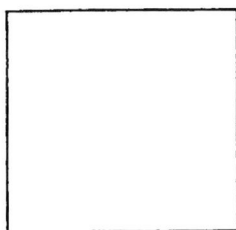

- ◆   Fold one flap over the   other, and you've made a pyramid or cone
  book. Don't glue in place until the children have finished writing on it!

Applications: *anything that goes in threes e.g. solid, liquid, gas; transparent, translucent, opaque*

- ◆   Turn the pyramid on its side,   and
  use it as a display book for scientific things:

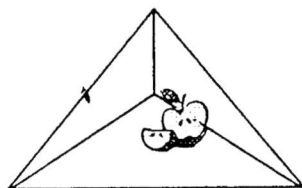

Applications: *anything that can be grouped, e.g things of the same colour, hard things, soft things, fruits, seeds etc., etc.*

- ◆   Display more things by putting them back to back, in twos or fours:

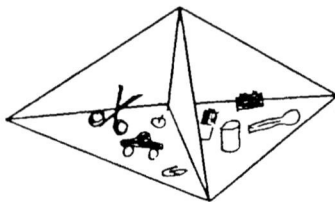

- ◆   Hang them from cotton to make a display:

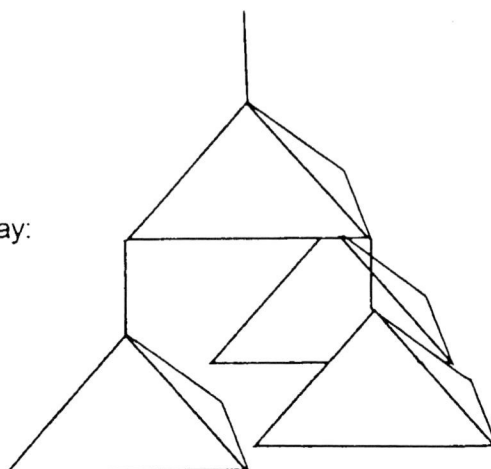

LINK Topic 14: Reading and making science non-fiction books

Flap book

4

- ◆ Fold a piece of A4 paper in half to A5, again to A6 and again to A7.
- ◆ Open out and fold lengthways.

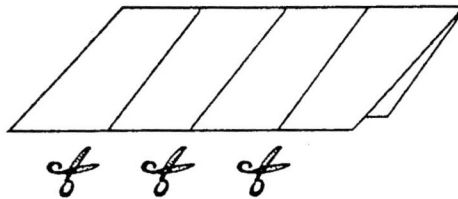

- ◆ Cut along the folds on the front of the book to make flaps.

Applications: *Questions on the front and answers on the inside; true or false; or cut one end off and use for any thing that goes in threes, e.g. solids, liquids and gases; transparent, translucent and opaque, possibly in a Venn diagram (see below)*

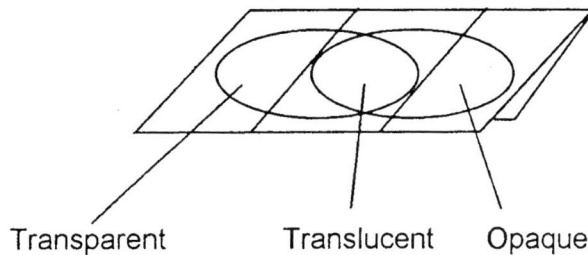

Transparent	Translucent	Opaque

or:

Things made of plastic	Things made of both	Things made of metal

Dangerous book (because if you go a stage further, they make those horrible little paper question and answer things they use in the playground on their fingers!)

- ◆ Cut a square of paper from an A4 sheet.
- ◆ Fold along both diagonals.
- ◆ Open out and fold each corner into the centre.

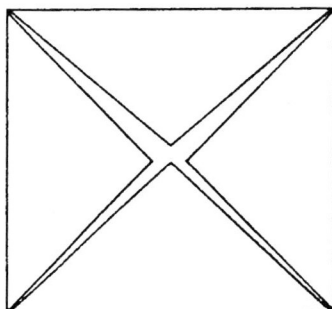

Applications: *Famous scientist biographies, Life cycles of plants, animals, humans, another way of recording your investigations (question and prediction, method, results, conclusion), cut each flap up the middle so you've got eight flaps for the phases of the Moon.*

LINK Topic 14: Reading and making science non-fiction books

Science

BOOK AUCTION

My favourite book was

By

1

Science

BOOK AUCTION

My favourite book was

By

1

LINK ▷ Topic 15: Writing in newspaper style

Stats News

This Month: COLONIAL PROGRESS

February 24, 1998 / Volume

THE WORLD GOES STATIC FOR FRANKIE

Only last night a remarkable discovery was made. A man named Benjamin J Franklin discovered an incredible invention called static electricity.

Franklin , his wife and his darling children have been working on this for many , many years unfortunately his wife is not here to join him she died in 1774 but Franklin says she is still in my heart every moment of the day.Franklins wife was devoted to his work and was willing to help in any way. If it was not for her he might of failed.

Franklin has fought his way through problems and has beat them all.For instance he once only worked in a broadsheeting company for a paper called The New England Courant he started this job in 1721 and if you were thinking that he was rich he was just as poor as me and all you lucky readers.

Overall I say three cheers for Frankie hip,hip,hooray, hip, hip, hooray hip, hip, hooray.

Thank you

ADVERT

NEW soap that   keeps static away from your clothes. SPECIAL OFFER

FREE tub and washing board.

PRICED AT $ 7.50

Reporter

Damien Hall

White Cottage

The Cliffs

Dear Children,

My husband, Mr Grinling and I have a problem that is pecking away at our patience.

Everyday I prepare Mr Grinling a delicious lunch but everyday those hungry seagulls eat my appetising treats. What can I do to stop these brazen birds? I have even tried mustard sandwiches, but now even they do not work. So I need your help.

Have you any ideas on how to stop the seagulls nibbling Mr Grinling's lunch? –perhaps a seagull-proof basket, but how?

Please can you help us solve this troubling situation.

Thank you,
Mrs Grinling

YAXLEY PRIMARY SCHOOL, CAMBRIDGESHIRE

BASED ON THE STORY, *THE LIGHTHOUSE KEEPER'S LUNCH*, BY R. AND D. ARMITAGE (SCHOLASTIC)

LINK ▶ Topic 18: Biographical and autobiographical writing

Charles Drew

Charles Drew was a black scientist who lived in America. He was born on 3 June 1904, the oldest of five children. He lived in Washington DC which is the capital of the United States of America. His parents were Charles and Nora Drew. His father laid carpets for a living and his mother was a teacher.

Charles was an intelligent and energetic boy, not afraid of hard work. At school he achieved many honours in his work and was also an excellent athlete. He graduated from High School when he was 18 and wanted to go to medical school to train as a doctor. However, he was unable to go straight into medical school because his parents could not afford to send him. So he decided to take a job coaching athletes in order to earn and save enough money to go to medical school.

Six years later in 1928 he started his medical course at McGill University Medical School. Charles Drew was an excellent student. He qualified in 1933, receiving a 'Master of Surgery' qualification and 'Doctor of Medicine'.

Medicine was less advanced in those days and many of the things that we take for granted were not available to doctors and patients. One of them was blood transfusions. Many people died at that time because they lost too much blood. It was a very serious problem and many people were researching into this area. Advances began to be made into finding out how blood could be grouped and a man called Karl Landsteiner (a Nobel prize-winner) found out that blood could be placed into four different groups. We use these groupings today; they are A, B, AB and O. Do you know what blood group you are?

During his training Charles Drew became interested in the problem of collecting, storing and keeping blood. He made many important advances in this area and during World War II he was involved in setting up a military blood bank system which allowed donated blood to be stored until it was needed.

Gradually he became a leading expert world-wide and he was asked to set up a blood bank system in England. This was the foundation of the present Transfusion Service. However, although he, a black American, became Director of the American Red Cross Blood Bank, there was still racial prejudice. Many people believed that not only should black and white people be segregated, but also that the blood of white and black donors should be kept separate, even though we know human blood is the same whatever a person's skin colour.

For this reason Drew resigned from his post and returned to teaching medicine at Howard University. In 1950 at the age of 46, Charles Drew was involved in a serious car crash and was taken to a 'whites only' hospital. Because of the colour of his skin, he was refused treatment and turned away. In need of a blood transfusion he was taken to the nearest 'black' hospital, but tragically died on the way.

The person who had helped to develop the blood transfusion service was denied use of the very thing he had created because he was black.